The Clinic of
Donald W. Winnicott

Paediatric psychoanalyst Donald W. Winnicott is widely recognized as a remarkable clinician. Deprivation, regression, play, antisocial tendencies and "the use of the object" are part of the many clinical conceptions he conceived, and here Laura Dethiville explains each in a clear and precise way, highlighting Winnicott's originality and enduring relevance. *The Clinic of Donald W. Winnicott* offers all readers a glimpse of what Winnicott brings to the understanding of the human being, and will appeal to students new to his work, as well as practitioners looking for a concise overview of his work.

Laura Dethiville, psychoanalyst, member of the Society of Freudian Psychoanalysis (SPF), has been leading a seminar on Winnicott for 20 years. Her previous work includes *Donald W. Winnicott: A New Approach*.

The Clinic of
Donald W. Winnicott

Laura Dethiville

Translated by
Susan Ganley Lévy

LONDON AND NEW YORK

First published 2019
by Routledge
2 Park Square, Milton Park, Abingdon, Oxon OX14 4RN

and by Routledge
52 Vanderbilt Avenue, New York, NY 10017

Routledge is an imprint of the Taylor & Francis Group, an informa business

English Edition © 2019 Éditions Campagne Première, Paris

© 2013, Éditions Campagne Première, Paris

The right of Laura Dethiville to be identified as the author has been asserted in accordance with sections 77 and 78 of the Copyright, Designs and Patents Act 1988.

All rights reserved. No part of this book may be reprinted or reproduced or utilised in any form or by any electronic, mechanical, or other means, now known or hereafter invented, including photocopying and recording, or in any information storage or retrieval system, without permission in writing from the publishers.

Trademark notice: Product or corporate names may be trademarks or registered trademarks, and are used only for identification and explanation without intent to infringe.

British Library Cataloguing-in-Publication Data
A catalogue record for this book is available from the British Library

Library of Congress Cataloging-in-Publication Data
A catalog record has been requested for this book

ISBN: 978-0-367-02759-9 (hbk)
ISBN: 978-0-367-02761-2 (pbk)
ISBN: 978-0-429-39794-3 (ebk)

Typeset in Times New Roman
by Newgen Publishing UK

For Dalva

Contents

Acknowledgements		viii
Introduction: Winnicott and his clinical work		1
1	Therapeutic consultation	3
2	The squiggle	13
3	The father	25
4	The family	38
5	Antisocial tendency and deprivation	50
6	Aggression and destructiveness	68
7	Adolescence	81
8	Regression	96
9	The area of playing in the cure	113
	Index	124

Acknowledgements

With thanks to all who have accompanied the writing of this book:

To the participants in my workshop, whose questions added to my own thinking.
To Marie Lacôte, for her reactivity, competence and effectiveness throughout this work.
To François Lévy, for his support, advice and his patience.
To Marie Baldit, for the care taken with the updating of the bibliography.

Introduction
Winnicott and his clinical work

At the beginning of my essay *Donald W. Winnicott: A New Approach* (Dethiville, 2014), I maintained that it is impossible to define Winnicott's concepts. All we can do is describe them. They have a life of their own, and often all we can do is follow them, trying not to lose our way. This second work is a confirmation of this.

Winnicott was writing up his work all his life. His texts show proof of continual research, sustained by his intense clinical experience, the influence of the world around him and the events he was involved in.

The study of children evacuated from London during the Second World War led him to conceptualize antisocial tendencies and deprivation, two revolutionary ideas that are absolutely essential in understanding certain pathologies. Those troubled times enabled him to formulate many of his principal ideas on the importance of the family and the "paternal" father – or, should we say, he who is something other than a simple replacement of the mother. But Winnicott's use of language, the intermixing of inventiveness and facilitation/compromise that are so typical of him, often obscure the originality of that which he is trying to show us.

In the course of his work, we are able to discern how his thinking and practice become more and more personal. His development of "the use of the object" remains the culminating point of his research and, retrospectively, clarifies his whole thought process. Dare we say that practice constantly preceded theory? To study how he worked, to discover his incredible presence in consultations with his patients, whether adult or child – a presence that owed everything to his ability to "play", whether it be in the squiggle game with a child, or in the transitional space he constructed with his adult patients – are an incredible lesson for us.

This is the idea that we will develop in this book, by using clinical illustrations of Winnicott's work. Because to see how he acts in the playing environment within the cure will help us feel/live that which his theoretical explanation does not necessarily clarify.

Winnicott wrote: "It has meant that what I've said has been isolated and people have had to do a lot of work to get at it" (Winnicott, 1967: 39–40). This was the warning in my first book – we would have to persevere. This time I am more tempted to build the bridges and pathways, however fragile, which I hope will lead us to his rich and complex thought.

References

Dethiville, Laura. 2014. *Donald W. Winnicott: A New Approach*, London, Karnac Books.

Winnicott, Donald W. 1967. "D.W.W. on D.W.W.", in *Psycho-Analytic Explorations*, London, Karnac Books, or in *The Collected Works of D.W. Winnicott*, vol. 8.

Chapter 1

Therapeutic consultation

It has often been said that Donald W. Winnicott was an atypical analyst. Even today, he is often referred to as being first a paediatrician, and later a psychoanalyst. But he was not a paediatrician who turned to psychoanalysis: "He was a consultant in a hospital for children, whose work was transformed by his personal experience of psychoanalysis" (Dethiville, 2014: 21). This perpetual back and forth influenced his maturing years considerably. As he would attest later, "no analyst was a paediatrician, and no paediatrician was an analyst. For twenty to thirty years I was an isolated phenomenon" (Winnicott, 1990: 72).

In 1920, Winnicott completed his medical studies, specializing in children's medicine (at that time the paediatric specialist did not exist). In 1923 he was appointed head of the infantile medicine department at Queen Elizabeth Hospital for Children in Hackney. He was 27. He also directed the rheumatic and cardiac department of the London County Council.

Paddington Green Children's Hospital

At the same time, he obtained a hospital post at the Paddington Green Children's Hospital, where he worked for 40 years, in what he mischievously called a "department for the management of maternal and paternal hypochondria" (Winnicott, 2001: 52). In this department he treated children with various somatic disorders. These children, often very small, were of course accompanied by someone in the family, mainly their mothers, for their fathers were at work. We can find accounts at the very beginning of his work in his notes (Winnicott, 1931), clinical studies of such illnesses as chicken pox, encephalitis, enuresis, haemoptysis, heart murmur, or urticaria. The discovery of antibiotics totally changed the understanding of such life-threatening illnesses. In this same year he began a psychoanalysis with James Strachey. In 1927 he began training as an analytic candidate in the British Psychoanalytic Society.

His clinical consultations gradually evolved from paediatrics to infantile psychiatry with a psychoanalytical approach. With time, he worked increasingly less as a paediatrician and more as a child psychoanalyst, at the same time using his medical formation to treat somatic disorders. He often described himself as "a psychiatrist with paediatric formation", which enabled him to save the lives of young patients, when he detected an organic disorder and was able to refer them in time to the relevant specialist.

It was at the Paddington Green Hospital where he developed empirically a method of working which he called "therapeutic consultation", a term he invented to distinguish this psychoanalytical work from psychotherapy.

He saw children together with members of their family. This meant that often there were lots of people present – including brothers and sisters of the child and many students and trainees – which seemed in no way to affect his ability to establish a link with his patient.

"The first time I attended his consultation at Paddington Green Children's Hospital," wrote Anne Clancier,

> I was amazed at how easily D.W. Winnicott established communication with a child. That very day one of the children brought to his consultation refused all contact; he stood still in a corner of the room, silent, avoiding eye contact. Winnicott sat down on the floor a little way from the child, took a pile of square pieces of paper, and a pencil, while another pencil lay on the floor next to the pile of papers; Winnicott rapidly drew a curved line, commenting all the while on what he was doing; the child became interested, drew nearer, and then sat on the floor.
>
> Winnicott invited the little boy to complete the doodle, as if the conversation was already in progress. After a while the child drew a line on the same piece of paper; then Winnicott carried on with the drawing, commenting all the time. Then he took up another piece of paper and invited the child to start the game; he drew a curved line, which Winnicott completed immediately, then it was his turn to start a scribble on another piece of paper, which the little

boy completed, and so on, each one either starting or finishing the drawing in turn.

(testimony of Anne Clancier in Clancier and Kalmanovitch, 1999)

These therapeutic consultations took place in a spacious room – an important factor because the topological layout was essential to his staging of the scene, which took place in the presence of an attentive, enthusiastic audience (student nurses, trainees and junior analysts).

The testimony of Joyce McDougall

Joyce McDougall was one of these observers, and she has often said how impressed she was by Winnicott's clinical acuity. She liked to recount the following anecdote:

> A young Cockney woman came into the interview room holding a little boy by the hand, Bobby, aged about three. Winnicott made him sit down and gave him a piece of paper and a pencil so that he could draw. Then he asked the mother why she had come. She pointed at her little boy and said: "Doctor, he doesn't shit any more. Our doctor said that everything is fine in his body, and that we should see a specialist."
> "How long has it been?"
> "It's been more than two weeks now. Isn't that strange?" And she went on to talk about her other child, an older girl, her husband and her work as a caretaker.
> At one point Winnicott interrupted her and asked: "Tell me, Mrs X, how many weeks are you pregnant?"
> "Oh, doctor! How do you know? I haven't told anybody, not even my husband. Nobody knows!"
> "Except him, he knows!" he replied indicating the little boy, who was busy drawing large circles.
> Then he turned to Bobby and asked him "Would you like to know more about the baby in your Mummy's tummy?"
> "Oh yeah, I want to!" replied the little boy nodding his head emphatically. Turning to the mother, Winnicott said: "You don't have to tell your husband if you don't want to, but you could find time to tell Bobby, couldn't you? Let him touch your belly and tell him that there is a little brother or sister waiting to be born."

"I just have to talk to him, is that all doctor?"

Winnicott asked the mother to come back the following week.

Eight days later, Mrs X arrived and announced triumphantly: "Oh doctor, he shits, and shits and shits again. It's a real miracle!"

(McDougall, 2009: 25)

We can find an account of this by Winnicott himself, dating from this period (his biographers estimate that he had met with around 60,000 families during his 40 years of therapeutic consultations!). It concerns his publication *Therapeutic Consultations in Child Psychiatry* (Winnicott, 1996), which appeared shortly after his death and contained a remarkable preface by Masud Khan.[1] We discover on reading this work that the essential point was to "allow a process to take place until completion", a theme which he had already tackled in his article "The Observation of Infants in a Set Situation", more often called "The Observation of the Spatula Game" (Winnicott, 1984a). In this text he describes his systematic use of the tongue spatula, an item usually found on a paediatrician's desk, when facing young children (between 5 and 13 months) on their mother's lap. This shiny metal tongue spatula captured the interest of the child and implemented a typical behavioural sequence.

Winnicott describes in detail the different phases of the process (the moment that the child reaches out to the spatula, hesitates, then puts it in his mouth before finally rejecting it), but the most important thing for him was allowing the child to pursue and complete its experiment. In fact what was important was not what was happening, but that it had happened. It allowed a process to develop completely.

For diverse reasons, the majority of the children he saw at the hospital were not able to benefit from the traditional psychoanalytical cure at that time:

- Distance: his reputation meant many people had to travel sometimes hundreds of kilometres to see him in London.
- Expense: the families he saw at the hospital were often from a modest background.
- Availability: for example, in one of the famous cases recounted by Winnicott, the parents of little Piggle could only come to see him sporadically, since they had to make a long train journey.
- Cultural reasons: at that time, child psychoanalytic treatment meant four or five sessions a week.

An overture, in the musical sense

The initial contact with the family and the child was essential for Winnicott. For him, almost everything happened in the first interview. He wrote "In my child psychiatry practice, I have found that a special place has to be given for a first interview" (Winnicott, 1964/1968: 299). This conviction was based on two elements. First, he was convinced that every human being hoped that somewhere a solution could be found, and he argued that the symptoms shown were a sign of this hope.

Second, he was equally sure that a patient, child or adult, would come to their first interview prepared to believe that they would find help there, and be able to trust him. It was not impossible that these first interviews might lead on to psychotherapy. Winnicott maintained that the manner in which the first interviews took place would lead to the establishment of satisfactory psychotherapy, since the child concerned would have encountered "some hope of being understood and perhaps even helped" (Winnicott, 1996: 5).

For Winnicott, the therapeutic consultation he had imagined/thought of had a very clear objective, that of giving the child and the family the help they needed to enable the dynamic lifelong process to continue – a kind of kick-start to revive the blocked process. It was positive code of ethics for him. And his invention of a therapeutic situation that was as brief as it was essential, involving one or very few sessions within a necessarily short period/time frame, was a flexible way of responding to the child's need to be helped.

It was also a method of working that gave him great pleasure – he speaks of enjoyment, a practice which he compared to music, since he feels it is one thing to work to improve technique, and quite another to interpret the music. Just as he wrote "if they are a labour to read then I have been too clever; I have been engaged in displaying a technique and not in playing music" (Winnicott, 1996: 31). And since we also use this musical metaphor, we could say that the therapeutic consultation works like an "overture", in the operatic sense. The elements are put in place for the events to come.

From the start, in his consultations Winnicott asked himself how he could know what the child needs, *hic et nunc*. He insisted on the term "needs", which raises a problem for the French. In fact, the term "needs" in English is what I would rather translate as "what is a necessity". It has never been question of satisfying a need, or meeting a need, but to find out what is a necessity (Winnicott, 1996: 31). For a need, however primitive, is above all a relationship and calls for interaction.

So the immediately related question is: "What means do I have to respond in the most economic manner psychically, *hic et nunc*?" – a therapeutic project implying the idea of "caring", which means to take care of, care about, be concerned, that is to say to enter the same basic preoccupation as that of the internal attitude of the mother who, by her caring, establishes the foundation of the mental health of the infant.

Winnicott calls this internal process "primary maternal preoccupation", a strange psychic state, often quite marked, which pregnant women enter into during the last weeks of their pregnancy, and which can carry on until a few weeks after the birth. It is this particular psychic state which allows the mother to provide what is "needed" "at the right time".

His conception of the birth of the psychic apparatus justifies the Winnicottian argument that it is easier to cure madness than neurosis. Neurosis falls within the analytical cure. On the other hand, "madness" comes from the failure of primary environment. It has to do with ordinary life. Therefore, where children are concerned, he is not in favour of analysis at all costs (see Dethiville, 2014: 8).

In this discussion, Winnicott often compares analysis to an art. But, as he writes, he refuses the practice of art for art's sake. "An analyst may be a good artist, but (as I frequently asked) what patient wants to be someone else's poem or picture?" (Winnicott, 1992: 291). "Analysis for analysis' sake has no meaning for me. I do analysis because that is what the patient needs to have done and to have done with. If the patient does not need analysis then I do something else" (Winnicott, 1984b: 166).

Moreover, he thought that what the children he saw in his consultations required in the first place was the re-creation of the "good enough" environment that they needed, whether it be provided by parents or social workers. He wanted the child to be able to "use" his family environment once more – meaning here, use as in use of the object. And in this work, he aimed to be more therapist than psychoanalyst, which led him to declare that it was more difficult to be a psychotherapist than an analyst.[2]

Using the environment

In his introduction to *Therapeutic Consultations in Child Psychiatry*, Winnicott sets the benchmarks that determine a good therapist:

One would rather have a really suitable person for doing this sort of work than an ill person made less ill by the analysis that is part of the psycho-analytic training. Of course it can be said that if one has been ill oneself one has greater sympathy with ill people, and that to be convinced of the value of reaching to the unconscious is to have experienced it. But somehow, it would always have been better if we had not been ill and in need of treatment.

If only we knew how to select properly we should know how to choose those who are suitable for doing the work that I describe in this book even when psycho-analytic training is not available. For instance, one can say at once that there must be evident a capacity to identify with the patient without loss of personal identity; there must be a capacity in the therapist to contain the conflicts of the patient, that is to say, to contain them and to wait for their resolution in the patient instead of anxiously looking round for a cure; there must be an absence of the tendency to retaliate under provocation.

Also, any system of thought which provides an easy solution is of itself a contra-indication since the patient does not want anything but the resolution of internal conflicts, along with the manipulation of external obstructions of a practical nature which may be operative in the causation or the maintenance of the patient's illness.

Needless to say the therapist must have professional reliability as something that happens easily; it is possible for a serious person to maintain a professional standard even when undergoing very severe personal strains in the private life and in the personal growth process which, we hope, never stops.

(Winnicott, 1996: 1)

The second point is about making the child capable of using his environment, or of making him capable *once more* of using it. In fact Winnicott had the very original idea that the family background, when it can be relied upon, remains the best place for the child to develop. And he tried to avoid perturbing the relationship the child had with his parents, so that he could help restore it. This was what he called "double therapy".

When we read his therapeutic consultations, we are struck by the extreme respect and tolerance he showed to parents, some of whom, from an outsider's point of view, were far from perfect. It is far removed from the trend which held sway in France to look for something to blame, when the parents were systematically accused. This meant that sometimes the parents were so affected, so traumatized after the first interview that the contact with their child became even more compromised, and they were even less able to ensure "the average expectable environment".

On the contrary, Winnicott relied a great deal on the parents, whom he continued to support at a distance, if he felt it was necessary, to give the child the container he needed to continue the maturing process. Claude Geets stated that "for the parents to be able to take on this task, it is not necessary that they themselves possess rock solid mental health, but there needs to be complete availability for the child's needs, particularly by the mother" (Geets, 1981: 39). And what is important is not that the parents should necessarily understand what was happening, but that they should be helped to find the adequate behaviour. At the same time, Winnicott is not naïve and he talks quite clearly of cases where it is necessary to separate the child from his or her parents. For example, when the mother is in a state of organized chaos "a chaotic state of affairs has been set up and is steadily maintained, no doubt to hide a more serious underlying disintegration that constantly threatens" (Winnicott, 1989: 390).

Or again when the child is confronted with the depression of one or other of his parents, without any mediation. His language is even chilling when he talks of these cases: "The point may be that there is no possible relief for this girl till her parents had died and she was established as an independent unit" (Winnicott, 1986: 74).

> It is a terrible thing and yet it is true, that sometimes there is no hope for the children till the parents have died. Psychosis in these cases is in the parent, and its grip on the child is such that the only hope is the development of a false self.
> (Winnicott, 1986: 74)

He also always insisted on the fact that "the child's illness belongs to the child". He contended that a child can find the means to develop normally in spite of unfavourable factors in his environment, where he might be ill even with "good care". He emphasizes what he felt was the essential faculty of the human being to be able to move towards health spontaneously, if given that possibility.

As we have already mentioned, the third basic axiom which sustains his work in therapeutic consultations ensures that if opportunity is given in the proper and professional way, the client will bring and display (though at first in a tentative way) the current problem or the emotional conflict or the pattern of strain which obtains at this moment of the client's life.

(Winnicott, 1986: 74)

And so, during the therapeutic consultation something will happen that Winnicott calls "the sacred moment", a precious moment that, if not spotted, will be lost forever.

This idea came to him after many years of practice. He was astonished when a child he was seeing for the first time would reply to the question "Did you dream last night?" by "Yes, I dreamed of you" (Winnicott, 1996: 7). In this way, for a brief, passing moment, he "fits the preconception" of a child who had been prepared by his parents "to go and see the doctor". He states that it is at this very moment that he plays the role of the "subjective object". "What I now feel is that in this role of subjective object, which rarely outlasts the first or first few interviews, the doctor has a great opportunity for being in touch with the child" (Winnicott, 1996: 4).

His personal style, very much an expression of his creativity and the man he was, can be seen in the way he enters into contact with the child. He uses the squiggle game, which calls upon an inimitable technique, often misunderstood. This technique is dealt with in the following chapter.

However we should bear in mind what he says about children and playing: "The playing child inhabits an area that cannot be easily left, nor can it easily admit intrusions. [...] What matters is the near-withdrawal state, akin to the *concentration* of older children and adults" (Winnicott, 2005: 51).

These quotations open a field for thought relative to his findings using this technique.

Notes

1 It is commonplace these days to slate Masud Khan and consequently attack Winnicott who, after having been his analyst, entrusted him with important editorial responsibilities. However we cannot ignore the merit of Khan's account of Winnicott's clinical work.
2 I came upon this idea in a work by Octave Mannoni. Twenty years ago, he regretted that "we in France have taken a different path". This leaves us wondering about the impact that has had on today's deviations.

References

Clancier, Anne and Kalmanovitch, Jeanine. 1999. *Le Paradoxe de Winnicott, de la naissance à la creation*, Paris, In Press.

Dethiville, Laura. 2014. *Donald W. Winnicott: A New Approach*, London, Karnac Books.

Geets, Claude. 1981. *Winnicott*, Paris, Editions Universitaires Jean-Pierre Delarge.

McDougall, Joyce. 2009. "D.W. Winnicott, trente-cinq ans après", in *Les Lettres de la SPF*, no. 21.

Winnicott, Donald W. 1931. *Clinical Notes on Disorders of Childhood*, London, Heinemann, or in *The Collected Works of D.W. Winnicott*, vol. 1.

Winnicott, Donald W. 1964/1968. "The Squiggle Game", in *Psycho-Analytic Explorations*, London, Karnac Books, or in *The Collected Works of D.W. Winnicott*, vol. 8.

Winnicott, Donald W. 1965. "Effect of Psychotic Parents on the Emotional Development of the Child", in *The Family and Individual Development*, London, Tavistock, or in *The Collected Works of D.W. Winnicott*, vol. 5.

Winnicott, Donald W. 1984a. "The Observation of Infants in a Set Situation", in *Through Paediatrics to Psychoanalysis*, London, Karnac Books, or in *The Collected Works of D.W. Winnicott*, vol. 2.

Winnicott, Donald W. 1984b. "The Aims of Psycho-Analytical Treatment", in *The Maturational Processes and the Facilitating Environment*, London, Karnac Books, or in *The Collected Works of D.W. Winnicott*, vol. 6.

Winnicott, Donald W. 1989. "Effect of Psychotic Parents on the Emotional Development of the Child", in *Through Paediatrics to Psychoanalysis*, Lausanne, Payot, or in *The Collected Works of D.W. Winnicott*, vol. 5.

Winnicott, Donald W. 1990. "A Personal View of the Kleinien Contribution", in *The Maturational Processes and the Facilitating Environment*, London, Karnac Books, or in *The Collected Works of D.W. Winnicott*, vol. 6.

Winnicott, Donald W. 1992. "Metaphsychological and Clinical Aspects of Regression", in *Through Paediatrics to Psychoanalysis*, London, Karnac Books, or in *The Collected Works of D.W. Winnicott*, vol. 4.

Winnicott, Donald W. 1996. *Therapeutic Consultation in Child Psychiatry*, London, Karnac Books, or in *The Collected Works of D.W. Winnicott*, vol. 10.

Winnicott, Donald W. 2001. "Family Affected by Depressive Illness in One or Both Parents", in *The Family and Individual Development*, Sussex, Brunner Routledge, or in *The Collected Works of D.W. Winnicott*, vol. 5.

Winnicott, Donald W. 2005. *Playing and Reality*, London, Routledge, or in *The Collected Works of D.W. Winnicott*, vol. 8.

Chapter 2

The squiggle

For French psychoanalysts, the term "squiggle" is indissociably linked to Winnicott, albeit without always perceiving its significance. Its translation has always been difficult and unclear. If we refer to the English term, we understand how Winnicott encourages the child to doodle, and these doodles in sequence constitute a squiggle; that is, literally, an illegible signature. Winnicott's squiggle was composed by two people, child and therapist, each continuing the freeform line of the other.

As in the case of the transitional object, strictly speaking Winnicott has invented nothing new. This kind of game, a mediation between two people, a creative interplay, was and still is very popular as an aid to the creation of a "shared" space. In *MetaMaus*, Art Spiegelman recounts that one of his favourite childhood memories is of the many squiggle games he played with his mother.[1] Once more, Winnicott picks up something that already exists and makes it his own, like finding a stone or piece of driftwood on a beach.

This is a perfect example of the found-created. The object is there, and it is the manner in which it is perceived and observed that gives it life. And the way Winnicott uses this popular game gives it a different meaning. Even in his private life, he loved squiggles and was constantly drawing them (Dethiville, 2014: 28). It is therefore not surprising that he chose a medium that was both familiar and natural for him. Playing the squiggle game was a way to come into contact with the child, and allowed him to take part in its spontaneity. It is for this reason that the technique is very difficult to imitate.

Moreover, Winnicott has always been particularly concerned that this technique should not deviate from its original substance, and for a long time he refused to write anything about this subject. We can find only two short papers dating from 1964 and 1968 (Winnicott,

1964/1968), in which he warns his readers against using the squiggle technique as a "gadget".

> Nevertheless I have hesitated to describe this technique, which I have used a great deal over a number of years, not only because it is a natural game that any two people might play, but also, if I begin to describe what I do, then someone will be likely to rewrite what I describe as if it were a set technique with rules and regulations. Then the whole value of the procedure would be lost. If I describe what I do there is a very real danger that others will take it and form it into something that corresponds to a Thematic Apperception Test.
> The difference between this and a T.A.T. is firstly that it is not a test and secondly that the consultant contributes from his own ingenuity almost as much as the child does. Naturally, the consultant's contribution drops out, because it is the child, not the consultant, who is communicating distress.
> (Winnicott, 1964/1968)

The process is more important than the technique

He also insists that it is the process that is important, and not the technique, since it is this which allows the adult to establish "communication" with the child.

> The fact that the consultant freely plays his own part in the exchange of drawings certainly has a great importance for the success of the technique, such a procedure does not make the patient feel inferior in any way as, for instance, a patient feels when being examined by a doctor in respect of physical health, or, often, when being given a psychological test (especially a personality test).
> I am absolutely flexible even at this very early stage, so that if the child wishes to draw or to talk or to play with toys or to make music or to romp, I feel free to fit in with the child's wishes.
> (Winnicott, 1964/1968)

> Perhaps a distinctive feature is not the use of the drawings so much as the free anticipation of the analyst acting as psycho-therapist.
> (Winnicott, 1999)

This technique is therefore inimitable, in the sense that it was his own. It is linked with his capacity for presence during the consultation. He says it gave him great pleasure, and evidently the children felt the same. He discouraged people who wanted to "do the same thing just to be like him", adding quite correctly that it was his own personality that was involved in the squiggle. He added that he freely played his own part in the consultation. So what does this involve?

Often, after asking the parents to return to the waiting room, Winnicott would say to the child: "Let's play something. I know what I would like to play and I'll show you." In front of him he had two piles of paper, one in quarto and one octavo, and two pencils. He said to the child:

> This game that I like playing has no rules. I just take my pencil and go like that ... You show me if that looks like anything to you or if you can make it into anything, and afterwards you do the same for me and I will see if I can make something of yours.
> (Winnicott 1964/1968)

It was then up to the child to start by drawing a line on the paper, a line which Winnicott completed. Then it was his turn, and then the child's and so on. It all went very quickly. In one consultation there could be 30 or more drawings. "Often in an hour we have done twenty to thirty drawings together, and gradually the significance of the composite drawings has become deeper and deeper, and is felt by the child to be a part of communication of significance" (Winnicott 1964/1968). What was important was the ping pong movement, the non-stop game between two people, back and forth, sharing the creativity.

There is a duality of creation in the *hic et nunc* of the session. As consultant, he was part of this co-creation, and generally this amused the children a great deal. As the game proceeded, Winnicott laid the numbered sheets on the ground, labelled "him", "me", "him", "me", etc. And the child could finally look at all the drawings, or he could choose one of them by saying "This is the one I prefer", etc.

There were thus two piles of paper on his desk, a small one of quarto, and a larger one of quarto cut in two. During one of his therapeutic consultations, the child laughed at his meanness in cutting the paper in half. In "The Squiggle Game", Winnicott explains the reason for this, and states that the size and shape of the sheet of paper are very important. He cuts the sheet in half so that the child doesn't feel that what he is going to do is very important, that it's just a game and he can let himself go freely. Each time that he reaches a crucial moment, the child reaches for the large sheet. This is a sign that calls for increased vigilance by the consultant.

Of course the drawing itself is important, but it has also led to a lively, rapid exchange, the intensity of which leads to a dream-like state, as he mentions. He insists on the fact that each child imposes his own rhythm. The child takes the lead in the game, and Winnicott merely follows him. The game progresses slowly, with occasional doldrums areas, as he calls them, which are periods of immobility, pauses during which the child seems to re-examine and weigh up the situation, wondering whether he can trust it – in other words whether he is confident enough to take the risk.

From this point of view, we can say that the same thing can happen during adult analysis: periods when we feel things stagnate, and which we put down to resistance, when it could be simply "ensuring solid support" in the mountain-climbing sense. We can also call it a time of re-evaluation, rather like putting a car's gear into neutral before going into first gear to drive off.

In a therapeutic consultation, this moment often results in a series of quite separate squiggles, or even the child's outright refusal to draw a squiggle, preferring a figurative drawing. And Winnicott lets things take their course and just waits. He gives the example of a little girl who refused to play the squiggle game, but who made a series of figurative drawings as fast as if they had been squiggles. However he felt this was not important, because what counts is not the drawing but the process. He considered that the goal had been achieved. "It's almost as if the child, through the drawings, is alongside me, and to some extent taking part in describing the case, so that the reports of what the child and the therapist said tend to ring true" (Winnicott, 1996).

> The important thing is to create an atmosphere where the child can feel free.
> The squiggles produced during these therapeutic consultations should be studied carefully, which is not easy, since the printing process blurs the lines most of the time. But if we take the time to study the drawings in front of us, one after the other, we can see how a dreamlike area builds up between the two protagonists. We could call it (and he does just that) a kind of daydream, a

modified conscious state, induced by the hypnotic and repetitive action of the game.

At a certain time, the child takes hold of a large sheet of paper, and he considers this moment to be a part of "communication of significance", which is the point when the analyst should comment on the drawing. "I wait until the essential feature of the child's communication has been revealed".

(Winnicott, 1996: 69)

In this particular context, it is not what we usually call an interpretation. In this situation, the analyst is not present as a person, but rather in his capacity as "subjective object", a simple sounding board. He makes it clear: "but the important thing is not my talking so much as the fact that the child has reached something" (Winnicott, 1996: 69). We must dispense with the idea to interpret it, because we must allow a creative space to unfold: this is where the vigilance of the therapist is so necessary. He adds: "In order to use the mutual experience one must have in one's bone a theory of the emotional development of the child" (Winnicott, 1996: 6).

We can understand how any inopportune intervention could alter the course of the session, for in such a situation, the child would have no alternative other than submission and defensive collusion, even massive rejection – which would in any case interrupt the process.

Winnicott gives as an example the fairly common representation in the squiggles of the snake. At that time – and even today – the snake was interpreted as representing the symbol of the penis. However, he noticed that the snake in the squiggle often represented a primitive self: the image the child has of itself, having no arms, no legs, nothing but a sinuous body. It was an indication informing him of the child's maturation process.

If we refer to his basic axiom that "if opportunity is given in the proper and professional way for a child or for an adult, then in the limited setting of the professional contact the client will bring and display (though at first in a tentative way) the current problem or the emotional conflict or the pattern of strain which obtain at this moment of the client's life" (Winnicott, 1996: 7), it is easy for us to convince ourselves that it would suffice for us to remain on stand-by, with respect and complete receptivity, and at the same time in a position of extreme vigilance. We should also induce a process of confidence and reflection so that at a certain moment something will emerge from the drawing that will take Winnicott and his young patient near to experiences which words cannot describe. "The patient surprises himself by the production of ideas and feelings that have not been previously integrated into the total personality."

In this intervening period in the transitional area something occurs which has the density of an actual experience. He confirms: "The rewards of this work are great because the consultant is able to learn in this way from the patient, and it is necessary for the consultant to be ready to learn rather than to be eager to pounce on the material with interpretations" (Winnicott, 1964/1968).

In other words, within the framework of the squiggle game, we need to keep a separation between representation and experience, between visible evidence and invisible psychic impressions, between an immediate reaction and a later significance. And what is more, we must be able to spot the particular moment the dreaming stage is arrived at. The squiggle created at this moment is revealed like the fragment of dreamed production, and at that moment Winnicott – the analyst – risks posing the vital question. For example, "Do you remember a dream you had when you were small?" to which the child almost always replies recalling a recurring dream he had in the past.

The sacred moment

There can also be a question concerning the child's transitional object. When we read the accounts reviewed in the book *Therapeutic Consultations in Child Psychiatry* – which are fascinating – we wonder what the signs were that allowed Winnicott to see that he had come to the Other Scene (Octave Mannoni's expression), to see that the "sacred moment"[2] mentioned in his introduction had been reached. When reading it, we are struck by its mystery and magic, but this is of course because we are not present in the room, and we are missing a large number of indications that inform us of what is taking place in this transitional area concocted between the child and the consultant. Among these, Winnicott talks of anxiety, or drive pressure, signs that signal the approaching moment when the child is on the point of entering a zone of distress. The child often also becomes agitated and occasionally touches his genitals.

At that moment, Winnicott takes a chance, he gambles. It is a vital moment. It is a risk that must be taken with great care, to allow the patient the possibly to disregard it, without hindering the process of personal creativity. For the role of the analyst as subjective object in this context is to contain the projections and give them back to the patient in a tolerable form. So every time the analyst takes a risk and the child indicates somehow or other that he is not yet ready to go this far, it is the responsibility of the analyst not to insist.

For we have to remember that it is the child calling the shots – as Winnicott continually reminds us – and if the child cannot play, all we have to do is make playing possible. In fact, at that moment the game acquires its full value by being reflected in the eyes of someone else. He writes, "This if reflected back, *but only if reflected back*, becomes part of the organized individual personality, and eventually this in summation makes the individual to be, to be found" (Winnicott, 2005: 64). This development is a version of that expressed in his article "The Mirror Role of Mother and Family in Child Development" and constitutes an essential aspect of that which we encounter in analysis, which consists of "giving back to the patient what he gives us".

We should in fact recall the way in which the infant tries from the very beginning to influence his environment, and the modulations by which he needs to be modified at the same time as he is modifying the world. If the child makes a move, the world must reflect this modification.[3]

The squiggle game, by its very format, seems to me to be similar to what happens at the very beginning of life. It produces an interrelation and an interaction which result in a to-ing and fro-ing movement, together with reciprocal modifications. The movement of one modifies the movement of the other, and modifies the ensemble itself.

For this reason, the squiggle constitutes a form of signifying communication which informs us what happened at an early period, a period without memory. It is a visual explanation of something that could not be thought of at the time, and which has remained without meaning. In that respect, it is close to what Freud felt about thought expressed in images, which is much more accessible than thought expressed in words. He also added that the dreamer forgot what would be inaccessible to him if he were awake.

In this way, the squiggle, like the dream, is a product of the subconscious, a product which seems at first formless, and which, in order to be interpreted needs the knowledge that comes from the transferential relation. It does not need interpretation, it needs to be created, "dreamed", produced. With the squiggle, something happens which is a psychic event in itself.

The squiggle as a signature

When Winnicott asks the child to doodle on the pages, this succession of doodles constitutes what he calls a squiggle, a kind of illegible signature.

We could possibly define the squiggle thus: the subject's signature, an undecipherable signature, until we give it meaning. Is the squiggle a subject's illegible signature, or an illegible signature for the subject?

When Winnicott begins to play the squiggle game with a child, he generally has very little medical history at his disposal. He prefers to approach the child with the maximum freedom of thought. This is very important to be able to understand the squiggle. He only saw the parents after the first interview with the child and in most cases, what was revealed in the game with the child was generally confirmed when he saw the parents.

In one of the chapters of *Therapeutic Consultations in Child Psychiatry*, he describes the game he played with Bob, aged six, and the integrality of the study is an example of the way he worked and what we mean by the term "gamble" mentioned above. Bob was a little boy who was diagnosed as being "simple" (a diagnostic rapidly dispelled by Winnicott), and suffering from enuresis and a difficulty to articulate, which made him difficult to understand. He had a two younger brothers, five years old and one year old.

The family had been referred to him by the psychiatrist who was treating the mother for the repeated fits of depression and panic attacks she suffered from. The father had also gone through depressive phases. Both of them had followed group therapy. Bob appeared first to be quite agitated. In addition, he was practically incomprehensible most of the time because he shortened his words. On the other hand, he communicated readily, and as Winnicott recounts, "it could really be said that he was full of some vague kind of hope" (Winnicott, 1996: 64).

At first he refuses to play the squiggle game, which he finds "too hard", and concentrates on figurative drawing. Gradually he takes part in the game very cautiously, but with moments of pause and immobility, doldrums areas after one or two squiggles which seem to have had an emotional effect. Then he feels at ease again and seems to enjoy the game. When we look at his squiggles, one after another, we struck by his constant addition of eyes in the shapes he draws, although Winnicott states "at this stage I had no idea that his putting in the eyes had significance, but in the critical drawing it made sense" (Winnicott, 1996: 64). By this remark, he indicates clearly that the therapist is keeping pace with the child, never getting ahead.

It's the appearance of Humpty Dumpty in the drawing – the little nursery rhyme figure so beloved of English children – that puts Winnicott on the right track: it was the lack of holding experienced at a certain time in Bob's infancy. But, as he says "it should be noted that in this work I do not usually made interpretations" (Winnicott, 1996: 72). For squiggle number 23, Bob asks for a bigger piece of paper. And he draws "a big hill, a very big one, a big mountain. You climb up there and you slip; it's all ice. Have you a car?" (Winnicott, 1996: 78).

Winnicott writes "From this I felt sure he was telling me about being held, and about being affected by someone's withdrawal of cathexis" (Winnicott, 1996: 79). Winnicott is certain that a crucial moment has arrived, and so asks the child if he dreams of similar things. Bob replies:

> It was last night or another night. If I see it I cry. I don't know what it is. It is a witch. It's horrid and has a wand. It makes you pee. You can talk but you can't be seen and you can't see yourself. Then you say "one, one, one" and you come back.

The word pee does not mean urine here. "No, not wee-wee! It means disappear. When the witch 'pees you' he makes you vanish" (Winnicott, 1996: 79). Then he draws himself in bed, having this nightmare and recounts something which really happened, when he fell downstairs. His father was at the bottom of the stairs. He picked him up and took him to his mother. He felt better.

At that moment, Winnicott takes a risk: he draws a maternal figure holding a baby and then scribbles the baby out and, when he is about to warn of the danger that the baby will be dropped, Bob grabs the sheet of paper, smudges in his mother's eyes and says "She goes to sleep".

"I now had his drawing illustrating the holding mother's withdrawal of cathexis" (Winnicott, 1996: 93). He adds: "I now put the baby on the floor in my drawing, wondering how Bob would deal with the archaic anxiety associated with falling for ever." Bob says:

> No, the witch came when the mother shut her eyes. I just screamed. I saw the witch. Mummy saw the witch. I shouted

"My Mummy will get you!" Mummy saw the witch. Daddy was downstairs and he took his penknife and stuck it into the witch's tummy so it got killed for ever, and so the wand went too.

This was the last drawing, and Winnicott writes: "Bob was ready to go. He seemed very satisfied with what had happened, and his excited state had calmed down." Afterwards, while Bob joins his father in the waiting room, Winnicott has a talk with the mother. She tells him about the periods of depression she suffered when Bob was little. Whereas the panic attacks appeared after the birth of the second child. At that point she started psychotherapy.

Winnicott asks "How did you first become ill? In what way did your depression show itself?" The answer was clear. "I kept finding myself going to sleep while I was engaged in doing something." Bob was 14–16 months when these symptoms started. It was impossible for her to handle the situation at that moment. The panic attacks started shortly afterwards, and Bob was faced with his mother's radical withdrawals when she fell asleep with him in her arms. He was no longer sustained by his mother's gaze. And since he didn't exist in his mother's eyes, he didn't exist at all! Winnicott emphasizes that

> the work of this therapeutic consultation is made more interesting by the fact that this boy did not use words at three years old, that he had a learning difficulty, and that he was generally considered to be "simple" by paediatricians, by school authorities and by the parents. It is unlikely that Bob could have told me what he did by verbal reply to verbal question.
>
> All details of experience had been retained and have been subjected to classification, categorization and collation, and to primitive forms of thinking. It is to be presumed that as a result of the work of therapeutic consultation this complex organization around a traumatic event became transformed into material that could be forgotten because it had been remembered.
>
> (Winnicott, 1996: 87)

As we can see, drawing the mother with the baby scribbled out in her arms is a risk he takes. It could quite well not have worked. By introducing this idea, Winnicott is "fishing". For his part, Bob might not have seen it and could have ignored it, without the defensive reaction that direct interpretation would have provoked. We must not forget that by the strategy he worked out using the squiggle, Winnicott was going against the child psychoanalysis practised by the Kleinians, as much by his view that it was a game as by the absence of direct interpretation.

His idea of a game was revolutionary at the time. In English there are two distinct words: *game* and *play*. *Game* refers to something organized, according to rules; while *play* is something spontaneous, moving in an unrestrained manner. Winnicott stresses that he uses the term *playing* to designate the verbal form, the actual playing. According to him, by concentrating too much on the content of the game, psychoanalysts have forgotten that:

> the natural thing is playing, and the highly sophisticated twentieth-century phenomenon is psychoanalysis. It must be of value to the analyst to be constantly reminded not only of what is owed to Freud, but also of what we owe to the natural and universal thing called playing.
>
> (Winnicott, 2005: 60)

Playing is a therapy in itself. At the same time it is in the transferential process, and the fact of being looked at by someone else gives a game like the squiggle all its value.

Of course there is an age for playing squiggle. The game is evidently not possible if the child is too young. In the case of a five-year-old patient of his, he states that he was "not sure that it would work with a child of this age".

Things become complicated with the onset of adolescence. Winnicott proposes a combination of squiggle and verbal squiggle. But using a drawing often allows the adolescent to feel more relaxed, and above all freed from observation by another person, which he can feel as an intrusion. It is a form of protection to keep one's eyes fixed on the paper, protecting the core of the self, which has to remain "incommunicado". In this way, the consultation with Patrick (Winnicott, 1965) was conducted between squiggle and verbalization, since verbalization could only be achieved through the process of the squiggle game.

The last point that we must emphasize, and which we find each time in *Therapeutic Consultations in Child Psychiatry*, as in the case of Bob, comes from the fact that most children seem to need one last drawing – a drawing that allows them to reintegrate and to leave behind the chaos of the session.

The squiggle is not a magic key, it is a means. The principle is that the psychotherapy takes place where the area of the child and that of the therapist overlap. The squiggle game is therefore an example of the way in which this cross-communication can be facilitated.

Notes

1 He relates how one of them drew lines haphazardly on a sheet of paper, which the other had to complete, to make something of it. This encouraged him to develop his visual imagination, and it remains engraved in his memory of childhood.
2 This "sacred moment", according to his rather strange expression, is that moment when the consultant is perceived by the child as a subjective object.
3 I refer to the work of Daniel Stern and François Roustang. I dealt with this question in Dethiville (2014).

References

Dethiville, Laura. 2014. *Donald W. Winnicott: A New Approach*, London, Karnac Books.

Winnicott, Donald W. 1964/1968. "The Squiggle Game", in *Psycho-Analytic Explorations*, London, Karnac Books, or in *The Collected Works of D.W. Winnicott*, vol. 8.

Winnicott, Donald W. 1965. "A Child Psychiatry Case Illustrating Delayed Reaction to Loss", in *Psycho-Analytic Explorations*, London, Karnac Books, or in *The Collected Works of D.W. Winnicott*, vol. 7.

Winnicott, Donald W. 1996. *Therapeutic Consultation in Child Psychiatry*, London, Karnac Books, or in *The Collected Works of D.W. Winnicott*, vol. 10.

Winnicott, Donald W. 1999. "Letter to L. Joseph Stone, 1968", in *The Spontaneous Gesture*, London, Karnac Books, or in *The Collected Works of D.W. Winnicott*, vol. 8.

Winnicott, Donald W. 2005. *Playing and Reality*, London, Routledge, or in *The Collected Works of D.W. Winnicott*, vol. 8.

Chapter 3

The father[1]

For a long time, Winnicott has been frequently reproached by French psychoanalysts for not giving enough place to the father figure in his theory – and I must say this disregard has not completely disappeared today. They are mistaken, but the consequences are devastating. The phrase is repeated like a slogan: "In Winnicott's theory there is no father, there is no symbol function." This allows them to discredit his work without taking the trouble to study it further.

J.B. Pontalis summarized, and criticized this very French position, which claims that in Winnicott's work the father is conspicuously absent, that it is constantly about the role of the mother, and that we hardly ever see a reference to libido. And he challenges this approximation.

In Winnicott's works, the reference to the paternal function is both essential and implicit. In fact the father is present all the time, on the side-lines. He is ever-present, in numerous clinical annotations, by small phrases here and there. For example:

> The young mother needs protection and information, and she needs the best that medical science can offer in the way of bodily care, and prevention of avoidable accidents. [...] She also needs the devotion of a husband, and satisfying sexual experiences.
> (Winnicott, 1957: 127)

We must admit that this is not bad coming from someone accused of not talking of sexuality.

To convince ourselves of the importance of the father in Winnicott's work, all we need to do is carefully read *Therapeutic Consultations in Child Psychiatry*, or consult the cases in *Deprivation and Delinquency*, in which he relates the damage caused by the absence of fathers during the war. He goes back to the story of Robert, who was born when his father was mobilized. When the parents came to see him, Robert was nine years old and manifested important symptoms. As Winnicott relates, the beginning of Robert's relationship with his mother had been perturbed by the absence of the father. And he adds: "At the time the mother was at the mercy of everyone ... The mother is a good mother and with support (*her husband*) she would have started better with him (*the baby*)" (Winnicott, 1996a: 89).

Winnicott concentrated particularly on the mother–child relationship, since he felt that the foundation of what he called "healthy" lay there. Accordingly, his contribution to psychoanalytic theory naturally related to this first period, which is what leads his detractors to maintain that the father does not exist in his theoretical argumentation. Admittedly his theory is not that of the paternal function, like that of Lacan, but he does reflect on the essential role of the paternal figure, which we find in the final developments of an unfinished and unrevised posthumous text, in which we could almost say he is questioning Freud on the subject of *Moses and Monotheism* and the necessity for man to build one God, a duplication of the symbolic father figure.

Therefore Winnicott's theoretic contribution is situated in the early time of the beginning of the little human being, a time when the mother-environment is essential. But he affirms that when he refers to the mother, he always includes the father, he means the father too. For the mother is referred to as a psychic reality, i.e., with her man in her mind. At this moment it is she who guarantees the paternal principle.

And above all, it is important to point out that when he speaks of the father, it is on the assumption that the father is necessary by right, and not as a reduplication of the mother. He speaks of "the paternal father and not the standing-in-for-mother-father" (Winnicott, 1967: 578). For it is an essential role for the father to be he who allows the woman to be a mother and not only he who creates the meeting of gametes. Simply to be the biological father is not enough to "embody" the father. The father's role is to create the benign circle surrounding the mother and the child until integration is achieved.

The first text on the subject of the father was written in 1947, just after the war. Winnicott was a man of his time, however he was forced to admit that there was a tendency to relax the traditional rules in English society. He was not opposed to it, but he constantly insists on the fact that a child does not need the father to be a second mother. For what is important for him is that the mother should be helped and protected. "And then it may be that there are some fathers who really would make better mothers than their wives." Maternal males, says Winnicott, can be very useful. They make good mother substitutes, for example, when a woman has several children, or when she goes back to work (Winnicott, 1947: 82).

Nevertheless, he adheres strictly to the idea that when fathers become the mothers, it interferes to a large extent with their function as a father. But this can be open to misinterpretation, and has been misinterpreted, and women often felt betrayed, since it was as if Winnicott was saying that the burden of everything concerning the care of the child rested on their shoulders. Once more we are faced with a *quid pro quo* regarding the difficult comprehension of the paternal function: it is not a question of sharing the tasks, but of different *psychic positions*. And it's not that simple. A man can be very present in the mothering of a child, but unable to assume the symbolic paternal function that that child needs to be able to build itself.

Describing one of his patients, he wrote: "one could say that he is so maternal that one wonders how he will manage when he becomes needed as a male man and a true father" (Winnicott, 1996b: 208). And in the 1947 text "What About Father?", a text that at first seems rather dated, Winnicott describes the classic society at that time: the father goes off to work in the morning, the mother stays at home. We find here in simple, even naïve terms, the specific question of the father, the paternal function, and the signifier of the Name-of-the-Father (which we recall has nothing to do with the patronym).

At the beginning, the father is the "protective cover" who allows the mother to remains as long as she needs to in a state of "healthy madness", a kind of hyper-sensibility that the mother has to the needs of her new-born baby, a state he calls "primary maternal preoccupation" (Winnicott, 1992). It is a particular psychic state – a state that the environment has to respect and protect – which allows the mother, thanks to her identification to the baby, to provide "at the right moment" what is necessary. It is a kind of psychic "availability",[2] which permits her to be "more or less" adapted.

This special situation she finds herself in does not only depend on her own mental health. It is also influenced by her environment, which allows her to get through it while being protected. And here, one of the important roles of the father is to give her the possibility to remain introverted and egocentric for a while.

The role of the father in the early stages is therefore to protect mother and baby "from whatever tends to interfere with the bond between them, which is the essence and very nature of child care" (Winnicott, 1991: 17–18). He guarantees the protective cover which allows the mother to ensure the "holding" of the infant, whereas by the care he gives to the infant, he is more involved in the "handling" (a point which has been revealed in recent studies). The father–infant interaction is situated more often in movement and playing games. For example, we often see that a father will rock a baby faster.

To represent this situation, we can say that it is the mother who holds the infant and the father who contains everything. It is doubtful that at that moment it is about the life of the little human being, or "paternal function", but the establishment of a "container" so that the mother–infant relationship can constitute the reliable environment necessary for the establishment of the child's going on being.

During this period, if the father has to be maternal, he is showing consideration for the mother, for his partner. So it is the father who allows the mother to be a mother. It is worth pointing out that it is an essential role at the start. We have too often tried to deny it. It is not necessarily the biological father who plays this role. In certain societies, it is the female friends and relatives who give support while the father keeps his distance, until the young mother is ready once more to be a lover.

In the case of deep post-partum depression, or even of puerperal psychosis, it can happen that in the absence of help from other women in the family (mother or father or sister of the mother) the father has to take over the role of maternal substitute for a while, and not that of protector of mother–infant. The clinic teaches us that the consequences of this situation are not easy to predict.

This kind of situation also occurs when the mother has been prevented from playing her role due to her state of health after the birth. It is neither a depression nor a psychosis, but an obstruction caused by a complication with the birth or some other health problem.

The father as third person

There is, however, something so complicated in the mother–infant relationship (a mixture of love and hate) that it needs a third person to prevent "cannibalization", so that the fantasy of a return to a single entity can be psychically achieved, the mother thus keeping her child within in herself. The father represents this third person. Naturally this means that the father has his specific place. He establishes the triangulation, and at the same time he has to position himself in this triangulation without feeling excluded. Equally he has to be aware of eventual feelings of jealousy which can be provoked by the child who has taken his place as her imaginary child. And also his feelings of envy of the mother's maternity, the person whose place, basically, he would like to take. It is a frequent occurrence, and its importance is often underestimated. We can even speculate that it is one of the unspoken reasons why men show a certain opposition to breastfeeding even if, of course, the argument put forward is that of the fear of losing the breast as a sexual object.

Remember that not so long ago it was believed that sexual relations could "turn the milk"! Therefore the young woman who was breastfeeding was prohibited from sexual relations, which was one of the reasons babies were put out to wet nurses. We can even estimate that it was one of the main, unconscious reasons that underpinned the abandoning of breastfeeding until recent decades.

The other reason, just as unconscious in my view, is the maternal phantasm in young fathers who would like to be a "mother" for their child as perfect as their wife is.

One of my patients had just become a father. He was able to provide the bubble that protects the bubble for his child and his young wife, whom he loved tenderly. Everything seemed to go well "all for the best in the best of worlds", and everyone seemed to be in the right place in their world. The baby was himself cooperating well. He hardly cried, and very quickly slept through the night.

One day, my patient, whom I saw face to face, arrived exhausted at his session. He asked me straight out, "By the way, does it ever happen that a mother's milk is not enough, and we have to add a bottle?" I asked him to explain: he said he hadn't slept all night because the baby was crying a lot and the mother seemed to have no milk because "she had forgotten to drink enough during the day".

I imagined that the baby, who was not very old, but who was born a big, vigorous child, had cried because he was hungry. I shared my thoughts with him, and suggested that they could perhaps give him an extra bottle feed, but that in any case they ought to talk to the paediatrician. Then I saw a flash of desire in his eye: "So then I could give it to him?"

It was not only the desire to "mother" his child, but the mad longing to take the mother's place, for the mother to be declared insufficient (for she did not have enough milk) so that he could take over part of her role. Effectively, the idea of an additional bottle had been rejected by the young mother, who was attached to the fact that she was the one who could feed the baby, and so was irreplaceable.

She was a young woman, extremely involved in her career, and once the period of maternity leave was over, she knew that she would go back to a busy working life. Unconsciously, she surely felt menaced by her husband, whose maternal identification (to his own mother) was particularly strong.

After we had dealt with this question, each of them could find their place and, thanks to the advice of the paediatrician, the baby was fed by either one of them with an additional bottle of milk ... and he stopped crying at night.

The mother-environment

Another patient, father of a new-born baby, arrived at the session one day exclaiming "You shrinks, you have got it all wrong! The father has no significant place at the beginning of the baby's life. I've tried it out lots of times. The baby behaves the same way with anybody who is not his mother!" In his voice of course there was no mistaking his frustration, but perhaps also his relief at not having to embody a paternal position which he knew would be awkward for him.

We must remember that in this first period, the place of the father is already important. The baby recognizes his voice and identifies his special place in the world encompassing him. It is therefore wrong to think that at that moment the father is only a person, with no other meaning. Since the baby is at that moment part of the mother-environment, the place of the father in the psychic reality of the mother is decisive, albeit subtle. All of this is true in the very first period in the life of the baby. But gradually the child leaves the stage of absolute dependence and begins to relate to a whole, separate person.

Winnicott emphasizes the importance of the relationship between the parents, a relationship that is obviously going to lend a certain tone to what he calls "environment". He writes that the father "helps the mother to feel happy in her body and happy in her mind" (Winnicott, 1947: 114). Or even:

A child is very sensitive indeed to the relationship between the parents, and if all goes well off-stage, so to speak, the child is the first to appreciate the fact, and tends to show this appreciation by finding life easier, and by being more contented and more easy to manage.

As Lacan said, with humour, "the best thing a father can do for his child, is to love the mother".

It is difficult for the mother to leave some space for the father, and not at all obvious. She has to accept that the father should be able to "castrate" her from her child, or at any rate from a certain kind of relationship with her child. She has to accept the "law" of the father. It used to be preached in certain analytical circles in France that the father must lay down the law, which brought roars of anger from feminists. In fact, it is all much more subtle, and the current methods of parenting show that nothing is simple in this area.

The indestructible environment

What Winnicott has always insisted on is the necessity for an "indestructible environment" – an expression in which the term "indestructible" means "that which survives the hate and aggressiveness of the baby itself". What is important is that this environment must not be destroyed. It is the survival of this environment that enables the baby to feel secure and to go from relating to the object to using the object. So the support of the father not only makes the mother able to play her own role, it also allows the baby to experience and live destructiveness, since it is not dangerous to be destructive when there is something indestructible to attack. Perhaps here lies the key point: the child should be able to experiment his destructiveness without damage.

One of my young female patients had separated from her husband when their child was 18 months old. She shows no regret at this decision. She remained on good terms with her ex-husband, and her little boy, who is now four, lives alternate weeks with one and the other. She says that sometimes it is difficult for her to live alone with her child, but she cannot envisage returning to live with her former partner.

Once, at the beginning of the week, she arrived at the session completely amazed and full of questions.

During the weekend she had gone with her child to an important meeting in aid of the country of origin of her ex-husband. Of course he was there too and they spent the day together. What troubled her was how much better and stronger she felt as a mother. She naturally was happy to see how happy the child was in the company of both parents together. But she was talking about *herself*, of the calm and peace of mind she felt. She was not nostalgic about the past with this man – she had gone beyond that. It was just the presence next to her of that person, the father of her child, a presence that brought her calm and tranquillity, because someone had the role of container. "It's strange, I really felt better and stronger, I don't understand it but I had to mention it," she said, somewhat perplexed.

She is a young woman with very feminist ideas, raised by a feminist mother influenced by the events in France of May 1968. She had never realized how much the presence of a father could be so important for a mother. The father is the arbitrator, coming between the mother and the child. He is there to protect the mother from too much love or hate, becoming the object of this hatred himself, and so alleviating her anxiety.

It is less destructive to come up against one's father rather than the mother, for the mother always remains something of the subjective object that she represented for the baby. To attack the mother is to attack oneself, and at that moment it is fortunate to have a father who can act as a buffer for this hatred.

In *Fear of Breakdown*, Winnicott recounts the case of an adult patient who suffered from a reaction to the environment, where the model was adequate, composed of a weak father and a strong mother. He therefore had to control his impulses very early on, "before he was ready to do so on the basis of an introjected father". In other words, he became inhibited – and according to Winnicott, massive inhibition necessarily encompasses the creative gesture. "This meant that he became inhibited, unaggressive and non-creative" (Winnicott, 1968: 327).

It is one of the major points in Winnicott's work: to establish the link between destructiveness and the possibility of living one's life creatively. What he means by destructiveness is, in fact, the spontaneity of the *impulse*, the "going towards", which is not destructive at all at the start, but which will be recorded as such in the psyche of the child, due to the reaction to the environment.

The father, a complete person

It is the non-survival of the object that gives the child's spontaneous gesture its destructive characteristic. And if the third person, the father, is not there to protect the mother (from the child's point of view) or to put things right, the child cannot take the risk. And this importance of the third party increases at the same time as the hereditary tendency towards integration projects the baby forward. It is from the person that is the father that the child first learns something about a human being different from itself, and different from other human beings, for the father will be seen from the start as a whole person whereas the mother will be viewed first as an ensemble of part objects, a conglomerate of partial objects.

In "The Use of an Object in the Context of *Moses and Monotheism*" Winnicott puts forward the idea that the moment the infant feels himself a unit, he will use the person "of the father as a blueprint for his or her own integration" (Winnicott, 1969: 243). In *The Ego and the Id*, Freud evokes primary identification, this famous primary identification, to the *prehistorical father*, by which he is actually indicating the parents united by the child in a reciprocal inclusion. This identification is immediate, primary and comes before any relation to an object.

Winnicott writes:

> But I suggest that in a favourable case the father starts off whole (i.e. as father, not as mother surrogate) and later becomes endowed with a significant part object, that he starts off as an integrate in the ego's organization and in the mental conceptualization of the baby.
>
> (Winnicott, 1969: 243)

He claimed that children are fortunate when they can get to know their father, "even to the extent of finding them out" (Winnicott, 1947: 116).

In "What About Father?", he emphasizes that even if the father is not there all the time, he should be there quite often so that the infant can have the feeling that he is real and alive and well. It's what he calls "the father at breakfast, he who has survived nocturnal attacks". And so "it is safe to dream that father got run over, or to have a dream in which in symbolic form the burglar shoots the rich lady's husband in order to get at her jewel box". Otherwise "if father is not present then such a dream is too frightening, and leads to guilty feeling or a depressed mood" (Winnicott, 1947). This is how he insists on the *real* father. In France, we would probably say that it was the imaginary father, the one the infant invents and who he must mourn to be able to reach the reality of the father.

However, whatever we say, it is not the same thing if the father is or is not there, if he is a "loser" or a hero: "For there is a difference according to whether the father is there or not, is able to make a relationship or not, is sane or insane, is free or rigid in personality" (Winnicott, 1969: 242). We must also take into consideration many things involved with the image of the father and his destiny in the interior reality of the mother. The presence of a real father allows the child to develop by the multiple games of identification which unfold in the life of a human being, identifications and mechanisms of projection and introjection that help to build a personality.

Let's take one of the examples given by Winnicott:

> I knew a girl whose father died before she was born. The tragedy here was that she had only an idealized father on whom to base her view of man. She had not the experience of being let down gently by a real father.

Had her father been alive during her childhood: "to be felt by her to be ideal, but also to be found by her to have shortcomings, and to have survived her hate of him when he disappointed her" (Winnicott, 1947: 117), then she would have developed a more rounded image of men.

In another example regarding the constitution of masculine and feminine selves of a young adolescent girl, Winnicott relates that

> there was a father who at first was scarcely ever present, and then when he came to her home when she was a little girl he did not want his daughter's female self, and had nothing to give by way of male stimulus.
>
> (Winnicott, 1974: 94)

In this case, there actually was a *real* father, an ordinary man with his own problems of being faced with human sexuation. The work in analysis later was long for the young woman, in order to shed the garb of the imaginary father, and use the real father as a support to attain her true desire.

Winnicott insists on the fact that it is much easier for children to have both their parents:

> One parent can be felt to remain loving while the other is being hated, and this in itself has a stabilizing influence. Every now and

again, the child is going to hate someone, and if father is not there to tell him where to get off, he will hate his mother, and this will make him confused, because it is his mother that he loves most fundamentally.

(Winnicott, 1947: 115)

At any rate, it is far less destructuring to come up against the father than to the mother. Present-day adolescent pathologies prove the point. Since, in this long work of integration, the support of the mother by the father allows the infant to perform something very complex: integrate his destructive impulse with his love impulse, which, for Winnicott, is a fundamental moment in the evolution of the little human being.

And the result when things go well is that the child recognizes the reality of the destructive *ideas* that are inherent in life and living and loving, and finds ways and means of protecting valued people and objects from himself. In fact, he organises his life constructively in order not to feel too bad about the very real destructiveness that goes on in his mind. In order to achieve this in his development, the *child absolutely requires an environment that is indestructible in essential respects.*

(Winnicott, 1990: 94)

He leaves this task to the father.

And finally, we hardly need to insist on something that seems so evident for Winnicott, who always declared himself a faithful Freudian; the father is the father of the Oedipus complex, he who permits access to the symbolic. Winnicott does not re-examine this point at a theoretical level since the way has already been mapped out by Freud. However the subject recurs constantly in *Therapeutic Consultations in Child Psychiatry*. Thanks to the symbolic function of the father, the child progresses towards the internalization of the law and, first, the law of prohibition of incest. And the superego will inherit the Oedipus complex.

In France we have for a long time insisted only on the symbolic father, represented by the mother's speech. According to her argument, it is basically secondary whether the father is there or not. What counts is the signifier the "Nom du père"; that is, the existence of the father in the mother's speech. We see how, by dealing with the very first moments of psychic life, Winnicott offers us a different, but at the same time complimentary way of looking at things.

We have now an overview of the functions that Winnicott assigns to the father. They are all different and can often appear contradictory to each other if we forget that these functions occur at different stages in the evolution of the child. It is not easy to play all these roles in turn. So, is the father symbolic enough? And the mother good enough? That is to say, just what is needed?

To end on a lighter note: in 2006 the Museum of Mankind in Paris organized an exhibition entitled "The Thousand and One Ways to be Born" (*Naître ici et ailleurs*). We learned that in Normandy of the nineteenth century, the father used to wave his nightcap between his wife's thighs so that the "paternal scent" would encourage the birth of the baby. It was the scent of the father, his essence – like the essence of a perfume – which was called upon to enable the baby to leave his mother's womb. A nice metaphor!

Notes

1 This chapter is based on the text of a conference given in Sao Paulo in 2012.
2 François Roustang's wonderful expression.

References

Winnicott, Donald W. 1947. "What About Father?", in *The Child, the Family and the Outside World*, London, Penguin Books, or in *The Collected Works of D. W. Winnicott*, vol. 2.

Winnicott, Donald W. 1957. "The Mother's Contribution to Society", in *Home is Where We Start From*, London, Penguin Books, or in *The Collected Works of D. W. Winnicott*, vol. 5.

Winnicott, Donald W. 1967. "D.W.W. on D.W.W.", in *Psycho-Analytic Explorations*, London, Karnac Books, or in *The Collected Works of D. W. Winnicott*, vol. 8.

Winnicott, Donald W. 1968. "Clinical Illustration of 'The Use of an Object'", in *Psycho-Analytic Explorations*, London, Karnac Books, or in *The Collected Works of D. W. Winnicott*, vol. 8.

Winnicott, Donald W. 1969. "The Use of an Object in the Context of *Moses and Monotheism*", in *Psycho-Analytic Explorations*, London, Karnac Books, or in *The Collected Works of D. W. Winnicott*, vol. 9.

Winnicott, Donald W. 1974. "Fear of Breakdown", in *Psycho-Analytic Explorations*, London, Karnac Books, or in *The Collected Works of D. W. Winnicott*, vol. 6.

Winnicott, Donald W. 1990. "Delinquency as a Sign of Hope", in *Home is Where We Start From*, London, Penguin Books, or in *The Collected Works of D. W. Winnicott*, vol. 8.

Winnicott, Donald W. 1991. "A Man Looks At Motherhood", in *The Child, the Family and the Outside World*, London, Penguin Books, or in *The Collected Works of D.W. Winnicott*, vol. 3.

Winnicott, Donald W. 1992. "Primary Maternal Preoccupation", in *Through Paediatrics to Psychoanalysis*, London, Karnac Books, or in *The Collected Works of D.W. Winnicott*, vol. 5.

Winnicott, Donald W. 1996a. *Therapeutic Consultation in Child Psychiatry*, London, Karnac Books, or in *The Collected Works of D.W. Winnicott*, vol. 10.

Winnicott, Donald W. 1996b. "Autism" in *Thinking About Children*, London, Karnac Books, or in *The Collected Works of D.W. Winnicott*, vol. 7.

Chapter 4

The family

In "The Child in the Family Group", Winnicott relates the story of a little girl who had named her transitional object "family".

> I think that in this case there was a very early recognition of inadequacy in the parental relationship, and it was at an astonishingly early date that the child tried to remedy the deficiency that she perceived by calling her doll *Family*.
> (Winnicott, 1990: 132)

The parents of this little girl were divorced, and the family had been split up. For a long time she had kept alive the fantasy of reuniting what had been separated. This is a common occurrence in many children of divorced parents and in the clinic we observe with admiration the numerous strategies used by the human being to achieve this.

In this way, illnesses or accidents or, even worse, attempted suicide, can have the effect of reuniting at the "patient's" bedside those who had drifted apart. But fortunately most of the time there is no need to go to such extremes – birthdays, Christmas, weddings, academic success can have the same result, bringing together for a few hours the two essential figures in the internal theatre of each individual. And occasionally it can be their own children who undertake the task. So we see divorced grandparents reunited at the bedside of a sick grandchild, the years having erased the pain of separation, and made possible not a reconciliation (which would be sentimentalism) but rather a temporary reconstitution of the core entity.

So this little girl had named her transitional object "family". Let us try and imagine what she was saying here. To do so, we have to go back to what Winnicott wanted to conceptualize by this term, which was a product of his clinical work. This concept met with enormous success, such a success that he had to clarify the meaning: "It is not the object (thing) itself that I am referring to, but how it is used."

Because, with the transitional object, what we as outside observers can see is only the visible part of the iceberg, part of an infinitely subtle and complex process that marks for the child the construction of an intermediate area, which Winnicott refers to as a psychic area, a particular place that he was the first to name and theorize about, and which he referred to thus: "[an area for which] no claim is made on its behalf except that it shall exist as an area of rest for the individual engaged in the perpetual human task of keeping inner and outer reality separate yet interrelated" (Winnicott, 2005: 134).

Winnicott's idea of a transitional area is one of his most revolutionary steps forward, and we often do not appreciate enough the impact of this breakthrough and the change it brought about in analytical theory. And yet it is a profound reversal of the classic theory that opposed the internal psychic reality and the testing of reality.

This intermediate area of experience, which is not queried as belonging to interior or exterior reality, makes up the greatest part of the infant's experience. So Winnicott insists on the necessity of this third area, in between objectively perceived and subjectively conceived. But this place is, strictly speaking, found nowhere, being neither part of exterior nor interior reality. At the same time, it is our most important area, the closest to us, the point of contact closest to our "profound reality", the place where we really live.

Is this what that little girl wanted to express?

"It would be a truism to say that the family is an essential part of civilization. The way we arrange our families practically shows what our culture is like, just as a picture of the face portrays the individual" (Winnicott, 2001a: 40). And yet we note that there is no entry for "family" in the *Dictionary of Winnicott's Use of Words* put together by Jan Abram, nor for that matter an entry under "*famille*" in the *Vocabulaire de la psychanalyse* by Jean Laplanche and J.B. Pontalis.

The word "family" is not a psychoanalytic concept. It would seem that psychoanalysis has never been particularly interested in this idea, except for the Systemic schools like those in Palo Alto, or in the antipsychiatry movement represented by Ronald Laing and David Cooper.

And yet Winnicott constantly talks of the family in all the aspects of his work, just as we saw he did for the role of the father. For if "there is no such thing as a baby", that is to say it doesn't exist without the arms that hold it, and the eyes that contemplate it, etc., in the same way this entity (mother–infant) does not exist without the environment, without the others who make up the internal and external reality of the mother.

> Each individual needs to make the long road from being merged in with mother to being a separate person, related to mother, and to mother and father together; from here the journey goes through the territory known as the family, with father and mother the main structural features.
>
> (Winnicott, 2001a: 40)

This relational ensemble called "family" is without doubt the core from which the structure of an individual's personality takes shape. Once more, it is not just a question of "loved" or not, but a subtle and complicated game of interrelations between the different elements of this ensemble. In France, Jacques Lacan addressed the same question in *Les Complexes familiaux dans la formation de l'individu* (Lacan, 1984).

Both authors stress that the important aspect of what is forged for the human being is the significance of each child in the conscious fantasy of its parents. It is the place occupied in the fantasy of the parents, well before the birth, which will radically affect the psychic fate of the infant.

The baby comes into a world that existed before him, a universe made up of other humans, with their culture, their codes and their language, a universe where in theory his place is already inscribed. He originates from the desire of his parents, from their desire and their history, he finds himself "caught up in it" even before he can "configurate" this ensemble by his acts. He will find his place at the junction of these two genealogies, defined by the signifiers that preceded him in the transgenerational impact. This is how the infant finds himself facing the enormous task of encountering a world "at the same time strange and familiar, in order to translate it in the actual terms of his existence" (Roustang, 1994).

Just as he continually insists on the activity of the baby, the baby's part in the setting up of his relationship with the mother, Winnicott will always uphold the idea of active "work" by each infant, in the building of the family, its continuity and its unity.

The family, a singular place

> It cannot be too strongly emphasised that the integration of the family derives from the integrative tendency of *each individual child*. [...]

> This contributing in from each individual child may be forgotten until one experiences the shock of a child who is ill or defective, and for whom for one reason or another is not contributing in. One then observes how the parents and family suffer in consequence. Where the child is not contributing in the parents are burdened with a task which is not altogether a natural one – they have to supply a home setting and to maintain this setting, and to try to keep up a family and a family atmosphere *in spite of the fact that there is no help to be derived from the individual child.*
> (Winnicott, 2001a: 46)

For a long time I considered these phrases cruel and unjust. How could we reproach somebody for not having fulfilled his task, when he was physically or mentally ill? It was a long time before I could understand that it was not a reproach, but a description based on his enormous experience of working with families and children at the Paddington Green Hospital, some of which he writes up in *Therapeutic Consultations in Child Psychiatry*. This is often the case with Winnicott and it is a little disconcerting. All at once he outlines concepts which had not been elaborated up to now, but which were clinically evident. And I needed even more time to understand that what he was talking about, when it concerned the family, was the creation of a singular place in this transitional area of the found-created. We only find what we have created and we only create because we find. It is individual creative activity that defines a unique psychic reality.

> There is a home with parents and children enriched by aunts and uncles and cousins. This is just an observer's statement. For the five children in a family there are five families. It does not require a psychoanalyst to see that these five families need not resemble each other, and are certainly not identical.
> (Winnicott, 1990)

And this place, thus created, will be that of multiple identification and the hazards of the development of psychic structure. Winnicott is far from idealizing the family structure at all costs. He is neither naïve nor sentimentalist. He knows that the family is also the scene of hate and soul-destruction. "I know that our relations are often a nuisance and that we are liable to grumble because of the burden of them. We may even die of them" (Winnicott, 2001a). This is how he explains the decision he took, as a consultant, to keep a child with problems of development in the family home as long as was needed; if he had taken the child away from the very ill mother, she would have collapsed without the support that the child represented for her. This in turn would have affected the family unity, which would have put in danger the psychic balance of the other children. It is a debatable choice from an ethical point of view. It's as if he sacrificed this child to preserve the much-touted territory called family. Indeed, when he could finally separate this little girl from her mother – that is, when the family circumstances were different – the little girl very quickly continued an evolution corresponding more to her possibilities.

Obviously, Winnicott did not idealize the family. However he considered that the family structure is the privileged system in the psychic organization. In *Therapeutic Consultations in Child Psychiatry*, he maintains that, except in the cases where it is truly dysfunctional, the best place for a child to be treated is within its family. And this was the aim of his work during his consultations: to ensure that the child was able to *use* his family, either because up until now the pathology of the family had made it impossible, or because it had been the child who had been incapable of using it. So his work during these brief but intense interviews was aimed at making the child able to use its family structure.

This echoes what we have discussed above, the subject of the necessity of the child's participation.

> The strength of the family comes from its being a meeting-place between something that arises out of the relationship of the father and the mother, and something that drives from the innate factors that belong to the emotional growth of the individual child – factors which I have put together under the heading of a tendency towards integration.
>
> (Winnicott, 2001a)

In this way, when a child has had the time to create and recreate the family by playing, so that it is assimilated to internal reality, he/she is ready to use the family as a means to move towards a relation with wider social groups. It is from this foundation that he/she will be able to fly off to new horizons.

Of course Winnicott establishes here a parallel between the use the child can make of the family and the use the baby makes of his mother. These movements towards a wider world are for him "excursions" and "returns" – excursions that are only beneficial if a return trip is possible. I always associate it with the phrase "Past this limit, your ticket is no longer valid". This often happens to us. We can't go back, and we can't continue either – a kind of immobility, that he calls "doldrums"[1] in adolescence.

It is the capacity to return to the parents and return to the mother, to return to the middle or to return to the beginning, which makes the separation "a growth factor instead of a rupture in the personality of the individual". It is not necessary for the return to actually take place, it simply has to be possible, to be able to be dreamed of. Of course for this to be possible, the parents have to still be alive, the family has to be intact, there must have been neither separation nor death:

> It would seem to me to be valuable to understand that as long as the family is intact, then everything relates ultimately to the individual's actual father and mother. In the conscious life and fantasy the child may have got away from the father and the mother, and may have gained great relief from doing so. Nevertheless, the way back to the father and mother is always retained in the unconscious. In the unconscious fantasy of the child it is always on his or her own father and mother that a claim is made fundamentally. The child gradually comes to lose much or nearly all of the direct claim on the actual father and mother, but this is conscious fantasy. What has happened is that gradually displacement has taken place from the actual parents outwards. The family exists as something which is cemented by this fact, that for each individual member of the family the actual father and mother are alive in the inner psychic reality.
> (Winnicott, 2001b: 91)

Let us say once more, it means the parents in the internal reality, who can be very different from the external parents, those in reality.

And nowadays, the extreme diversity of the family constellation, with its divorces, stepfamilies, assisted procreation, and now the authorization of same-sex marriages and the possibility of adoption, all these factors challenge traditional psychoanalytic theory. We can no longer think of the individual psychic movements in terms of triangular relationships and of an Oedipus complex which would be an essential moment in the structuration of the individual. Or else we could say that this forces us to rethink the Oedipus complex.

Everything is registered in more mobility, playing, more flexibility, much more lability in the possible identifications. It is here that Winnicott's position becomes extremely valuable for our work, since he considers the territory called family as privileged territory, a territory and at the same time a temporal area which allows the process of maturation to develop optimally. As long as we keep our ears open, what our patients on the couch bring to us is subject to umpteen changes, is more vast, much more complex, and more varied than the Oedipus trilogy. Consequently, for a long time we have misunderstood crossed interrelations among siblings, the importance of the role of brothers and sisters and this, far beyond the habitual and banal fraternal rivalry, and well beyond the famous "complex of intrusion" developed by Lacan. For example, in large families when there is a big difference in age between the oldest and youngest children, the older children have a parental role, often closer to their siblings than the parents themselves.

One of my patients had a young uncle, hardly older than he was. This uncle had been brought up by my patient's mother, that is to say his elder sister. She had been an orphan for a long time, and had looked after her young brother until her marriage. This uncle had always figured in the fantasy of my patient as the eldest child of his mother, he who had taught her to be a mother. "In fact my mother had brought up three children: her brother, me and my brother," he explained. This phrase seemed to describe a simple family constellation, and it was a long time before I realized that behind it was the fact that he could not identify his active role in his mother-becoming-a-mother, because, in fact, *he* had been her first child, and he had been robbed of this active role. Consequently, in adulthood he could not recognize his role in loving relationships, which all failed, one after another. If I had not read Winnicott, I would never have made this connection.

There is another well-known fact that we must insist on: the existence of stepmothers and stepfathers permits the dispersion of the ambivalence associated with the subject of parents. Instead of feeling hate and love for one and the same person, we can project the hate on one and love on the other.

Loyalty and disloyalty

Winnicott introduces a new idea, that of loyalty and disloyalty. In fact he uses this term in the classical sense of loyalty to the king, meaning fidelity to a vow.[2]

What does it mean for him? It is all about how the child should be able to experiment with successive and continual separations and reconciliations without it destroying the relationship with one or the other of the family members: how he should be able to go from the mother to the father or vice versa, or from the mother to the nanny, or to the aunt or to the grandmother, without these excursions being experienced as disloyalty-infidelity. "It is in the family that we may hope to find this tolerance of what looks like disloyalty if it is not simply a part of the growth process" (Winnicott, 1990: 137–138). And according to him, it is the matrix of the games children play together:

> and in the games, the children of a family introduce all the strains and stresses which belong to this kind of experimentation with disloyalties, even including the perceived tensions and jealousies that exist among the grown-up people in the environment.
> (Winnicott, 1990: 138)

In a certain sense, he adds, it is a good way to describe family life in theoretical terms.

So for him, family games are a perfect preparation for life and for the real world in which these children, once grown up, will have to live, and above all, these disloyalties-infidelities make up a essential feature of life. "They stem from the fact that it is disloyal to everything that is not oneself if one is to be oneself. The most aggressive and therefore the most dangerous words in the languages of the world are to be found in the assertion: I AM" (Winnicott, 1990: 141).

Within the sibling group

We used to read children's stories depicting nasty stepmothers or stepfathers, which helped to idealize the mother, often deceased, and all the hatred could be projected on to the evil stepmother, potentially a murderess, like in Snow White or Cinderella. And since we cannot plunge the human being into a world solely made up of cruelty, and since in general the real mother is dead, there is nearly always a good fairy or godmother who takes on the qualities of gentleness, goodness, kindness and protection.

Nowadays, the real stepfathers and stepmothers bear the brunt of this diffracted hate, which protects the parent. It is not unusual that the opposite happens and that the stepmother (the woman desired by the father) inspires more admiration than the mother. And then it can all change again when further modifications to the family occur.

In the Cinderella story we also see how the malevolent daughters of the stepmother are jealous of Cinderella, and want to take away everything that means so much to her and, above all, refuse to grant their stepsister her rightful place in the family. Of course it is banal to stress that this represents ambivalent sentiments between siblings.

However, these same ties are often not taken into account enough in a traditional analysis or by traditional psychoanalysts, for whom the "norm" is to resolve the Oedipal conflict. And yet what happens within a sibling group, and this, dating from an early time of life, and far removed from the famous Oedipus complex, helps us more effectively from our position in the cure, provided that we choose to hear it.

Julie came to see me, referred by a colleague, who was a friend of her parents. She is a tall, pretty adolescent who takes great pains to explain to me that she feels fine, and that it is her mother who is anxious for nothing. Of course she wanted to be slim, like all adolescent girls, and she is on a diet and continues to lose weight, but, as she says "it's only an adolescent thing", and it is not serious, and it's really her mother who needs looking after.

She explains all this without aggression, strangely distant, as if she was not really concerned. She tells of how she was taken to see a psychoanalyst at the age of four, because of her fits of anger. "It worked," she says. "I don't lose my temper like that anymore and I am really someone quite easy to live with." She says this without any trace of irony.

I said to myself that her symptoms had effectively disappeared, thus suppressing any means of asking for help. And the start of adolescence awakens moments of auto-destruction, which put her in serious danger. And yet she denies any malaise and considers that what she is feeling is normal at her age.

Her parents were divorced, but everybody got along very well. Her father had remarried and she has a very good relationship with her stepmother with whom she is able to discuss things that she could not discuss with her mother. Her mother lives alone, and her overanxiety is a burden for the daughter, but apart from that everything is fine. She can only be positive with no possibility of ambivalence. She cannot be "disloyal". Officially she lives with her mother, but can come and go as she pleases between the two homes (in agreement with the adults). She has always been a good pupil, but recently the results at school have taken a nose-dive.

Apart from this small detail, everything is going well. Her parents are intelligent, respect her and give her a free rein. She has a younger sister she has always got on well with, and with whom she has always been complicit and supportive versus the parents. "We are alike. We are so close to each other that people used to think we were twins." I notice that she said "used to" but say nothing. It is the end of the session, and she leaves, relaxed, and agrees to come back again.

After the session, I let my mind wander. I get the impression that all is "too good to be true", as if she had presented me with the perfect clinical case of an ordinary adolescent, simply caught up in her multiple identifications, between a stepmother, the object of the father's desire – slim, elegant, professional – and a mother who is a little older, not elegant and not at all social: someone she does not want to resemble.

And I had in the back of my mind this "used to" in connection with her sister, and that sole visit to an analyst who had magically suppressed the symptom. I was obviously expected to do the same. Equally I had the impression that this eating disorder was far more serious than she wanted to admit and that she was slowly developing a severe anorexia. At the same time, the organization of such barriers against any aggressive intrusion meant that a possible cure might even be compromised.

In the course of the following sessions, I gradually learnt that just after her, a boy had been born who did not live long. The mother's grief was terrible, and to try to overcome it, the parents had very quickly decided to have another baby. The birth of this little girl had helped the mother overcome her grief.

Very quickly, Julie became very attached to this little sister, and she to her. I kept remembering the phrase "people thought we were twins". This way of abolishing the distance between them and thus all forms of otherness helped her to avoid any rivalry, to annul it, to enable her to remain in a dominant position. But above all, it served as a defence against an early depression, a primitive breakdown, perhaps at the time her mother was pregnant with the longed for baby boy.

During her childhood, this little sister had been the support she needed to keep going. But with the advent of adolescence, everything had changed, not for Julie but for her little sister. She began to prefer going around with her own friends, leaving Julie out, with no rampart against her depression. She collapsed.

The discovery of these facts, revealing a first disaster, was long, painful and very risky. Many times I thought I would have to protect her by a temporary hospitalization. I did not need to, since the parents, concerned by what was happening, ensured effective containment, and the sessions (on demand) gave her the holding that was missing

So she could finally "put this experience of primitive agony to the past tense", as Winnicott would say, "alas there is no end unless the bottom of the trough has been reached, unless *the thing feared has been experienced*" (Winnicott, 1989: 91–92). I am sure that I could never have understood the revelation in her first interview, if I had not recalled this theory of an earlier period. She might have left after only one or two sessions, and could have continued drifting to self-destruction, and perhaps worse.

I have chosen a fragment of this cure among the many examples that clinical work continually teaches us. For example, a brilliant young woman came to see me for her temperamental relational difficulties. The material presented immediately had something to do with a chaotic and unpredictable mother but quite soon there was underlying evidence of the impact on the psychic construction of my patient caused by the existence of a sister who suffered from a strange skin ailment, which necessitated her avoiding sunlight. The dynamic of the whole family was focused on this child, their way of life, holidays, etc., everything was dictated by the need to take this illness into account.

This transitional area called "family" could not be created by my patient, since her needs had never really been taken into account, overshadowed by the needs of her sister. She had very quickly taken refuge in an intense intellectual life.

Her present angry behaviour was an attempt to rule the world, just as her sister had succeeded in doing in the family. To ignore the impact of the reality of this illness on what had been her environment would have led to a block in the cure, or even, as in the case of Julie, to a submissiveness to dogmatic interpretation.

Therefore it was in this family environment that she created her way of facing the world around her.

Notes

1 Doldrums: to be in low spirits (not the "blues" or depression).
2 An example would be the expression "my loyalties are divided".

References

Lacan, Jacques. 1984. *Les Complexes familiaux dans la formation de l'individu (1938)*, Encyclopédie française, tome VIII. New publication in *Les Complexes familiaux*, Paris, Éditions Navarin.

Roustang, François. 1994. *Qu'est-ce que l'hypnose?*, Paris, Minuit.

Winnicott, Donald W. 1989. "Fear of Breakdown", in *Psycho-Analytic Explorations*, London, Karnac Books, or in *The Collected Works of D.W. Winnicott*, vol. 6.

Winnicott, Donald W. 1990. "The Child in the Family Group", in *Home is Where We Start From*, London, Penguin Books, or in *The Collected Works of D.W. Winnicott*, vol. 7.

Winnicott, Donald W. 2001a. "Integrative and Disruptive Factors in Family Life", in *The Family and Individual Development*, London, Brunner Routledge, or in *The Collected Works of D.W. Winnicott*, vol. 5.

Winnicott, Donald W. 2001b. "The Family and Emotional Maturity", in *The Family and Individual Development*, London, Brunner Routledge, or in *The Collected Works of D.W. Winnicott*, vol. 6.

Winnicott, Donald W. 2005. "Transitional Objects and Transitional Phenomena", in *Playing and Reality*, London, Routledge, or in *The Collected Works of D.W. Winnicott*, vol. 3.

Chapter 5

Antisocial tendency and deprivation

The concept of antisocial tendency and deprivation are new terms introduced by Winnicott to psychoanalytic vocabulary. As on many other occasions, he has forged these terms based on his clinical experience. This was how he worked. Something unknown would appear in his clinical work, something that had not yet been accounted for in the theory, he respected it and then tried to formalize it. Sometimes this would produce brilliant semantic findings but sometimes less positive phrases. However, we have to admit that there is often a lack of precision in the use of these ideas, a shortcoming that becomes a possible source of confusion and *quid pro quo*. This is particularly true of the "antisocial tendency", one of the most diabolical concepts of his corpus, especially for we French, for we must absolutely not confuse "antisocial tendency" and "delinquency" or "asocial act".

Let us begin by saying that delinquency is only one of the possible consequences of antisocial tendency, one of its destinies. The organized antisocial tendency is overloaded with secondary gain. In fact what complicates things is that, in his texts, Winnicott himself goes from the idea of antisocial tendency to that of asocial act – and vice versa – without it seeming very clear to him. So, for example, in 1967 he began a conference entitled "Delinquency as a Sign of Hope" (Winnicott, 1990: 90) by announcing that in fact he was going to talk about antisocial tendency. This doesn't help us make sense of it!

For Winnicott, antisocial tendency is not a diagnosis. It is a name he gives to a moment in the evolution of each individual. Once more, we have here a vital step forward for psychoanalysis.

Antisocial tendency is, he states, "the passage of a particular moment for every human being", a crucial moment, which he situates at the stage of concern, the moment when the child ceases to be ruthless. It is that moment when the child projects on the same mother the fusion of aggressive impulse and love impulse. In this passage, the child in his fantasmatic life experience attacks, sullies, robs the mother, creates chaos, and attacks the breast with greed. Often this stage goes unnoticed. However, Winnicott writes:

> the antisocial tendency can be studied as it appears in the normal or near-normal child, where it is related to the difficulties that are inherent in emotional development. [...] For the sake of simplicity I will refer only to children, but the antisocial tendency may be found at all ages.
>
> (Winnicott, 2012: 120)

We can see the manifestation of antisocial tendency at all times of life, even in old people: some running away, incontinence, violence can be interpreted in the light of this concept of Winnicott's.

At a later period, that is to say at a time when things are not only experienced in fantasy but acted out, it is antisocial behaviour that will reveal that the subject had experienced deprivation in childhood, and his behaviour will be the sign of a regression to this structural moment of antisocial tendency.

Winnicott gives credit where credit is due and reminds us that is due to John Bowlby that there is recognition of the relationship between antisocial tendency in individuals and emotional deprivation occurring at the end of the first year or during the second year, that is to say the period of "relative dependence". Bowlby had put forward this theory when working with children who had been hospitalized. Where there is antisocial tendency, we always find deprivation behind it, say both Bowlby and Winnicott. Let us state here and now, deprivation is not privation; this is an essential point and we must continually bear this in mind. We will come back to this more fully later, but we can at this stage quote Winnicott's definition of deprivation:

> There has been a loss of something good that has been positive in the child's experience up to a certain date, and that has been withdrawn; the withdrawal has extended over a period of time longer than that over which the child can keep the memory of the experience alive. The comprehensive statement of deprivation is one that includes both the early and the late, the pinpoint trauma and the sustained traumatic condition and also both the near-normal and the clearly abnormal.
>
> (Winnicott, 2012: 124)

Antisocial behaviour and deprivation

The first signs of deprivation are so common that they can pass as normal. This is the case with – and we often see this – the sudden appearance of imperious behaviour in a child. In the face of this the parents generally react with a mixture of submission and reaction. They imagine that it is part of the child's development and that "it will pass". However, Winnicott emphasizes that the way the child behaves has nothing to do with the manifestation of an externalization of infantile omnipotence, omnipotence which lies in the period of illusion, where it is question of psychic reality which *must* be experienced. At this moment it is "antisocial behaviour in reaction to what the child perceives as deprivation".

Other signs may appear like bed-wetting, running away, truancy, "a centrifugal tendency that replaces the centripetal gesture which is implicit in thieving" (Winnicott, 2012: 129), greediness, which is not the same as the term 'greed' in psychoanalytical theory. The greediness of the child or the adolescent cannot be compared to the instinctual claims of the baby. In fact the symptoms often occur when, after an initial *good enough* mothering, there is a failure of the environment in the second or third year, for example the separation of the parents, the birth of a younger child, the mother's hospitalization, a change of address, or a death that the parents must overcome – some of the many accidents in life which affect the quality of the environment.

Winnicott also considers that another symptom of deprivation, which we find in many of our adult patients, is the compulsion to go out and buy something. He adds that most analysts are powerless in these cases, since they are not able to think of it in terms of antisocial tendency. Therefore antisocial behaviour is the sign of an antisocial tendency fixed by the result of an experience of deprivation. At the root of this behaviour there is a cause other than the aggression inherent in each human being, an aggression which is a sign of good health. There is deprivation, which Winnicott states is a process that implies the environment. This change takes place in a period of the child's life when it begins to perceive the environment as being different from itself – it can thus situate the failure as coming from the exterior.

But paradoxically – as is often the case with Winnicott – the appearance of antisocial behaviour should be considered as the sign of positive evolution. It represents "hope", "the hope of finding what had been lost, to force the environment *to be what the infant had needed*" (Winnicott, 1996). If he has hope, it is perhaps a sign of something positive in his environment. It is at this stage that he hopes to rediscover the satisfactory state, which existed before the failure of the environment. A child who steals (in the initial stages) simply reaches back over the gap. He hopes to rediscover the lost object, the maternal concern or the family framework he has lost – or at least doesn't give up trying to reach it. It is in fact a kind of appeal, an appeal to the environment (Winnicott, 1996).

As we have already evoked, this antisocial tendency has many different forms, and is manifested by two important trends: on the one hand, stealing, where the child is object-seeking; and on the other, destructiveness, which is the search for environmental stability.

Let us go back to the process of "found-created" (Dethiville, 2014). The baby thinks that it has created the "mother-environment" who is there at the right moment with just a slight gap in time, which gives the child the illusion that a world exists corresponding (and answering) to his capacity to create. He sees himself as active in the satisfaction of his needs. Later on, stealing is a kind of "remake" of this process. It is not so much looking for the object as the capacity to create – as we often observe, the stolen object is quickly lost or damaged. In fact, during the process of stealing, the very second that he takes hold of the object, the child (or the adolescent) has the feeling that it is part of himself. He succeeds surreptitiously in experiencing once again his capacity to create the object. And it is that which is important: it is not so much the object as being reunited with the capacity to find-create.

We often hear it said that when a child steals, he is seeking the mother over whom he or she has rights, because he created her. This is the case, but it seems to me that what he or she is looking for above all is to experience their capacity to create once again. And to be able to do this, the child must go through terrifying experiences, afraid of what he thinks is his capacity to destroy. For the other important feature of the antisocial tendency concerns the "urge to destroy".

We are reminded that Winnicott was the only one to claim that at the beginning of life, it is not aggressiveness but a spontaneous movement that goes out into the world. This movement towards, this modifying infringement as I call it, modifies the world at the same time as it modifies the individual himself. However this transformation of the world can be perceived by the child as a destructive attack, if it gets this message from the environment. What should have been felt as an enrichment the child feels as something disintegrating.

Furthermore as there has been a "failure" in the mother's survival, the child tries and tries again to "enrich" its world, since it absolutely has to renew the experience of an object that can be attacked without being destroyed.

In everyday life we often meet this type of situation. We could call them the impingements, the "micro-traumas" of life – Winnicott calls them episodes of "sub-deprivation". Normally there are no important consequences, as long as they are mild and are "repaired", in the sense that the environment can allow the child such a repair.

Here we must take care to be precise, for it is a point that leads to much confusion. When Winnicott talks of repair, it is not the mother with regard to the child. According to him, the gesture of tenderness that most of the time follows the failure of the environment is a way for the parent to try to compensate, but the importance lies in the idea that this rapprochement gives the child the illusion that he has just repaired the mother he had attacked in his fantasy. Such repair allows him to imagine he is active in the creation of his world. At the same time as he perceives the destruction, he is given the chance to repair it. During this process his phantasmagorical destructiveness loses its danger.

> It will be seen that in every household there are minor instances in which a child has become a deprived child in a small way and is cured by the parents who (quite naturally and without instruction) feel that this child needs a phase of spoiling, as it is called. Spoiling here means giving a limited and temporary opportunity for the child to regress to dependence and to a maternal provision which belongs to an age that is younger than that of the child at the moment.
>
> (Winnicott, 1996: 217)

But if the occasion is missed, due to events in the environment or happenings in life, then the situation will, as he says, remain "frozen", just as Lacan uses in his language the terms "frozen" signifiers. The child can no longer connect the calm mother and the excited mother, the mother-environment and the mother-object. This disunited excitement constitutes a reservoir likely to explode later in antisocial or even delinquent behaviour, or be contained by a defensive inhibition, which will petrify any emotional life and any creativity.

One of my patients was unable to show any emotion, even though he was what we call a nice fellow. He was incapable of loving. When he was three, his mother had died while giving birth to a little girl, who did not survive the birth. He was then brought up by a loving stepmother, who gave him everything. What had inhibited him in his capacity to love was the impossibility he found himself in to "repair the mother" after the intense aggression he had felt for her during the pregnancy she had "inflicted" on him. She had disappeared (this is what he said) in a moment of violent rage and of love just as violent. At the time, he could not connect the two feelings. To love had become too dangerous, since it would bring about the death of the object.

In this sense, we can consider antisocial behaviour to be an attempt at self-cure, like an appeal to a structure, an environment that allows integration of these movements, to unite that which had been undone during an experience of deprivation. The child has suffered an unthinkable agony and extreme confusion at that moment. He has gone through a period of distress, apathy, stagnation, depression – a moment that often goes completely unnoticed. The child is calm, almost too good. He is "neutral", writes Winnicott. He has lost the ability to play, in the sense Winnicott gives to this activity. Often the transitional object has lost all interest for him. In fact, the child is depressed, but no one realizes it. When, for one reason or another,

> hope begins to appear, and this means that the child, without being conscious of what is going on, begins to have the urge to get back behind the moment of deprivation and so to undo the fear of the unthinkable anxiety or confusion that resulted before the neutral state became organized. This is the very deceptive thing that those in care of antisocial children need to know if they are to see sense in what is going on around them.
> (Winnicott, 1990: 92)

Now, if we add that the antisocial way of life is an attempt to keep a distance from psychic suffering, we can understand that the child who destroys, breaks things, who steals or runs away, is provoking his entourage and forcing the environment to react. This appeal for help must be seen as a sign of an immense malaise. It is a demand, admittedly made in a noisy, unpleasant way, but still a demand. In this way it is important to spot this symptom during consultations with children, and not to confuse it with the hyperactivity of a manic child or the agitation of a child who is trying to psychically animate his depressive parent.

Recuperating an adequate environment

Once more, Winnicott disconcerts us by asserting that in young children, psychoanalysis alone remains powerless in face of the task of treating the antisocial tendency. He states: "It is the provision of child care which can be rediscovered by the child, and into which the child can experiment again with the id impulses, and which can be tested" (Winnicott, 2012: 315).

In *Therapeutic Consultations in Child Psychiatry*, approximately one third of the cases he describes concern children with antisocial tendencies. Each time, Winnicott relies on the family framework, which he expects to take over at the end of the consultation.

> Research into the antisocial tendency is best carried out on the simpler cases or in those cases tackled early, and especially in those where there is an environmental provision which can adapt itself to improvements that may take place in the child's character and personality as a result of a consultation.
> (Winnicott, 1996: 215)

He is referring here to pre-pubescent children. If, later on in adolescence, the antisocial tendency develops into one form or another of delinquency (which, as we remember, is only one possibility) the management of the situation will be different and a foster home may be found necessary. But even when this solution is resorted to, it is a psychotherapist or educator who is called for, or someone capable of accompanying the child in this painful journey. "The antisocial way of living was a way of keeping despair at a distance. But now this moment of deprivation has to be relived, because there is no end to it unless the bottom of the trough has been reached." The antisocial child will only pull through if: "someone has gone back with him and enabled him to remember by reliving the immediate result of deprivation" (Winnicott, 1990: 98). And here all the force of the transferential relationship intercedes.

In "D.W.W. on D.W.W.", Winnicott (1967) confides that frankly he needed "a certain number of years before he realised something that was in fact very simple", that there were two kinds of deprivation. One of them is expressed in terms of object loss, while the other can be described as the loss of a framework that protects against attack. In other words, it is the loss of the mother and the loss of the father – the "paternal" father, not the father who may replace the mother (as we have seen in Chapter 3). Of course this same duality occurs in antisocial trends: on the one hand, object seeking, and the other, the destructive tendency, and everything which that implies.

And finally, Winnicott describes the case of Philip (six years old) to illustration his contention that, for a young child, it is not so much psychoanalysis that cures him as the recuperation of the lost environment. This account is very instructive in the way it teaches us about the antisocial tendency, regression and the respect of the syndrome. The analyst says he chose this case in particular because psychoanalysis could not be envisaged.

Treatment by regression

Winnicott had three interviews with Philip, after which he, as we might say, passed him over to his parents, having explained to them what was needed for their child. The boy's mother had an aversion to psychology, which as Winnicott says,

> proved to be valuable to me in my management of the case, since I was able to rely on her feelings and on her native or intuitive understanding of human nature and not on her sporadic reading and thinking. [...] Later on I described what the boy of her, not in terms of the needs of a psychiatric case but in terms of the need of a normal infant, explaining that the boy would need to be allowed to go back to being an infant in relation to her, so making use of his newly founded home. Thus we avoided having to instruct her against her will in psychopathology.
> (Winnicott, 1953: 104)

The parents had come to consult on the advice of their paediatrician, because Philip had begun a series of thefts which had incurred his exclusion from school. He writes:

> It was almost by chance that I was in a good position to give help at the very beginning and before a moral attitude towards the boy's delinquency had had time to become organised, and before symptom intolerance had developed to the extent of producing panic therapy.
> (Winnicott, 1953: 104)

The interview with the parents convinced Winnicott that they had shown that they were capable of creating a real home, even though it had been terribly shaken by the war. The father was in the army and had left for the front at the beginning of the war, when Philip was two. He left the family home at that point with his brother and his mother. He was four when they moved back again. However, the family life that had been interrupted by the war only really resumed when the father left the army, which was shortly before the consultation. "The children's possessions were necessarily scattered, never all available at one time, and any one object was liable to become lost" (Winnicott, 1953: 105).

At the age of six, and after the birth of a little sister, and a tonsillectomy, Philip started to steal. At about the same time he became very untidy and started to dress himself badly.

During his interviews with Winnicott, Philip talks about what he calls "the dark days", the moment of deep depression after the deprivation and the way he "hallucinated" his mother when he was separated from her at the birth of the sister. He and his brother were looked after at that time by an aunt and uncle. "I would see my mother cooking in her blue dress and I would run up to her, but when I got there she would suddenly change and it would be my aunt in a different coloured dress" (Winnicott, 1953: 111). During this period, he was greatly helped by his elder brother, who continually told him: "It's going to end, it's going to end."

In this way, he had already experienced a first deprivation when he was two, at the moment his father left for the army, the moment when he had also probably lost the contact with his worried and depressed mother, but after which he became rather calm and withdrawn. His mother said that she found it more difficult to establish contact with him than with his brother. Shortly afterwards, the separation caused by the birth of the sister had reactivated this first failure of the environment. He found himself helpless in face of the aggressive feelings he had for the mother who had "betrayed" him in this way, and this was why he had to hallucinate her – he had to recreate her to be sure that he had not destroyed her.

The father's return home and the change in the family's life (the father had bought a farm) had modified the environment and raised his hopes, hence the appearance of his antisocial behaviour.

In this way, writes Winnicott, he was ill and had to be allowed to become worse – and the parents, who were supported by correspondence with Winnicott, were able to give him this opportunity. Winnicott continues:

> I now come to the illness that the boy had to have during which the parents provided him with asylum. It can be briefly described. This child needed my personal help, but there are the many cases in which the psychotherapeutic session can be omitted, and the whole therapy can be carried out by the home. The loss is simply that the child fails to gain insight, and this is by no means always a serious loss.
>
> (Winnicott, 1953: 94)

Philip was accepted at home as a special case, an ill child needing to be allowed to become more ill. By this I mean that there had been a controlled illness and this was to be allowed to come to full development. He was to receive that which is the right of every infant at the start, a period in which it is natural for the environment to make active adaptation to his needs.

What it looked like was this: Philip became gradually withdrawn and dependent. People said he lived in a fairy world. His mother described how he did not so much get up in the mornings as change from being in bed to out of bed, simply because someone dressed him. This is a lay method of saying that the boy was in a somnambulistic state. On a few occasions the mother tried encouraging him to get up but he was quickly reduced to tears of distress and she abandoned all encouragements. At meals he gathered the utensils around him and ate alone, although with the family. He seemed uncivilized, taking big gulps of bread, and eating the jam first. He would eat everything that was there mechanically, seeming neither to want food nor to reach a stage of having had enough. All through the meal he was in a preoccupied state.

He went downhill steadily, becoming less and less able to live in his body or interested in his appearance, but he kept in touch with the enjoyment of body by watching his greyhound for hours on end.

His gait became uncoordinated, and towards the bottom of the regression he progressed by a hop-skip technique, arms waving like windmill sails, or by a series of lurchings, as if propelled by some crude agency living within the self, certainly not walking. While progressing in this way he made noises which his brother called "elephant noises". No remark was ever made about his many oddities and eccentricities and bizarre behaviour patterns. He had the cream from the one cow, and also he figuratively skimmed the cream off the homeliness of the home. On occasions he would come out of this state for an hour or two, as when the parents gave a cocktail party, and then he quickly returned to it.

Once he went to the local "Hop" and there his unusual attitude to girls came to the fore. He danced a little, but only with a very odd and overweight girl known as "the galleon", assumed in the locality to be mentally defective. A radio thriller became an obsession during this period, and his life revolved round this and watching the dog.

Then the bottom was reached. He was always tired. He had increasing difficulty getting up at all. He became a bed-wetter for the first time since infancy. At last I have reached the symptom which made me choose this case for description. The mother got him up, between 3 and 4am each night, but he was usually wet. He said to her: "I dream so vividly that I got to the pot." Also at the time he was addicted to water, drinking to excess. Of this he said: "It's such fun, it's delicious, it's good to drink." All this took about three months.

One morning he wanted to get up. This marked the beginning of his gradual recovery, and there was no looking back. The symptoms peeled off and by the summer (1948) he was ready for a return to school. This was delayed, however, until the autumn term, one year after the start of the acute phase of illness. There was no return, after the first psychotherapeutic interview, either of the wizard or of the voice, or of the stealing.

On the return to the same school Philip picked up quickly, and there was no difficulty about living down a reputation for thieving. Soon the headmaster was able to write the usual letter one expects, asking what was all the fuss about, the boy being perfectly healthy and normal. He seemed to have forgotten that he had expelled him a year previously.

> At 12, Philip went to a well-known public school, rather a tough one, and at 14 he was reported to be 5ft. 5in., broad in physique, manly by nature, always out of doors, and good at the usual games. He was reported to be one year ahead of his age group scholastically.
>
> (Winnicott, 1953: 116)

Winnicott used this case history in a lecture aimed at illustrating his position over the method of treating bed-wetting like a symptom which it was not possible to eradicate by behaviour analysis. At the same time, it is a wonderful example of the appearance of antisocial behaviour following a return of hope. After three interviews with Winnicott, this child was cured by a regression which was made possible within the framework of the family.

The case of evacuated children

The situation will prove more difficult with an older child or with an antisocial adolescent, for adolescence is indeed the sensitive time when an antisocial tendency can crystallize into delinquency. Winnicott himself tells how

> Up to a certain date in my career I avoided the antisocial case both in my clinic and in my private practice, knowing that I had nothing to offer, and that the clue was missing. I simply saw antisocial children in a routine way in order to provide notes for a court.
> After a certain date, however, I found myself able to offer some kind of a service for those cases that came to me in which the antisocial tendency was the main symptom. Since then I have allowed myself to become involved in many of the cases that can give a great deal of trouble even when everyone is trying to be helpful and tolerant.
>
> (Winnicott, 1996: 216)

This evolution in his way of seeing things occurred at the same time as he was developing his ideas on deprivation, which was an entirely new concept he introduced into his theoretic vocabulary. This term first appears in connection with mothers in a paper given on the BBC in 1939 ("Deprived Mothers"). He addresses mothers whose children had been evacuated from the cities due to the war. This is an episode that is not well known in France. Since England had never been occupied, we have the image of a civil population that was spared this. However, there are a few films that show life under the bombing. In his film *Hope and Glory*, John Boorman describes his childhood memories. Even though everything had been organized for him and his sisters to leave London for Australia, his mother cannot bring herself to allow her children to leave, changes her mind and keeps them with her. He remains in London for part of the war, in a district which is heavily bombed. His father had joined up. There were hardly any adults to turn to. He and his friends spend their days wandering around the town, playing in the ruins, destroying everything that was still standing, discovering sexuality, sometimes coming across a dead soldier, until their home is destroyed by fire and what is left of the family move to the country to stay with an atrabilious grandfather, with whom he establishes a strong bond.

The decision by the mother to keep her children with her for this (in hindsight) short period protects the children from the trauma of separation. This is evidently the message in the film. Thanks to an atmosphere of tender "holding", there is no devastating trauma caused by the reality of war.

It is otherwise in Peter Brook's film *The Lord of the Flies*, based on the book by William Golding. Following an aircraft accident, a group of children find themselves trying to survive, alone, on a desert island. Very soon acts of barbarity take place between the protagonists. The book has been the object of much psychoanalytical study in terms of the id, ego, and superego. When we know that the aircraft was carrying "evacuated" children, children who were being moved away from London and who had been brutally separated from their families, we have a completely different interpretation of the book. The savagery and cruelty take on a different significance.

From 1 September 1939 (the date of the outbreak of the war), the English government set up a vast plan of evacuation. It was necessary to protect the lives of the children living in the big cities – in particular London, which was subjected to heavy bombing. The children were therefore sent away to the country to foster homes, and for those who could not adapt to this, to "wartime hostels".

This evacuation scheme concerned primarily the poorer families, since the well-to-do families generally were able to find other means of keeping their children safe. The evacuation was "voluntary", but it was accompanied by what we would call today "intense media coverage". Psychological pressure was huge. Even the royal family was active in this propaganda. Afterwards, many parents felt that their agreement had been to a certain extent extorted from them. Indeed, after the first wave of evacuations, there was real opposition from parents, and the second evacuation in 1940 was deemed a partial failure.

This was how in the space of a few days, 800,000 children, accompanied by teachers and responsible adults, were sent away by train to destinations unknown to them or their families. This manifest lack of preparation accentuated the feeling of insecurity for both children and parents. It was a violent traumatism for the families and for the children. The parents were torn between the desire to protect their children and the suffering of having to be separated from them for an undetermined period of time, and this at a time when travel was not as easy or widespread as it is today. Many children went for long periods without seeing their parents. The separation was traumatic for the whole country, but the return home was just as bad. They had to "get to know each other" again, and it was far from easy.

The testimony of former evacuees is often found in English literature and shows the intensity of the upheaval caused. Whether the placing in the foster family was a success or not (some children were mistreated in foster homes, while others, especially the little ones, became strongly attached to their foster families and suffered a second traumatism at being separated from them), the scale of the disaster was enormous for families and children alike.

> Even before the establishment of this scheme, Winnicott, John Bowlby and Emmanuel Miller had alerted the authorities to the danger of separating children from their families. If these opinions are correct it follows that the evacuation of small children without their mothers can lead to a very serious and widespread psychological disorder. For instance, it can lead to a big increase in juvenile delinquency in the next decade.[1]

Winnicott in particular developed the idea that what was important for the small child was the permanent secure environment represented by the mother. The real danger was less important. What was important was the emotional reaction of the mother. "During air raids, the babies were not afraid of the bombs, but they were affected as soon as they felt their mothers start to panic." He did the best he could, having been appointed consulting psychiatrist for the government's evacuation scheme. As such, he supervised the hostels created in Oxfordshire for difficult children who could not be placed in foster homes. He also supervised the many social workers who had been appointed to look after the foster families. During the war, he spent half the week in Oxfordshire, which, incidentally, meant he was hardly present during the controversial discussions which were rocking the British Psychoanalytical Society, although he did his best to attend the scientific meetings.

Many children and adolescents caused problems in the families where they had been placed, and in the neighbourhood: truancy, stealing in gangs, burning of haystacks, and general nuisance. Some of them went back to the cities, but most stayed in the foster homes and "became a real nuisance unless they could be offered residential management in hostels". Needless to say, the general public was alarmed to see these young savages running wild in the countryside. The English government, engaged in fighting a war, had to find a solution to the problem they themselves had created, in spite of the warnings.

This was when the wartime hostels came into being, which in turn became places of therapy. For many young people, the antisocial tendency, which pre-existed but was relatively calm, rapidly turned into delinquency due to evacuation, which reactivated the primary deprivation. Most of these children came from broken homes, or just before evacuation had experienced a near break-up, and they did not need a substitute family. "They needed a satisfactory primary home experience" (Winnicott, 1947: 57).

Once the war was over, the return home of the children was far from straightforward. "I come across children who cannot remember what their mothers are like, and who only remember with difficulty the names of their brothers and sisters" (Winnicott, 1945b: 45). The separation had consequences, which were sometimes irreparable. The homecoming was not always easy. The fathers were not back from the war, and some of them would never return. Once again, Winnicott far from the gentle picture we paint of him, is lucid about the unconscious feelings of the parents. "Their return means that your life will be richer, but less your own. [...] At times you will wish all of them back again in billets" (Winnicott, 1945a: 52).

Thus, during and after the war, Winnicott discovered the effects of what will later become his theory of deprivation – not a happy term, we must admit, but no worse than the term "antisocial tendency". As we have seen above, for Winnicott, deprivation indicates the loss of a satisfactory environment in the period of relative dependence that precedes access to autonomy. The case history regularly reveals a primary period when the environment allowed the infant to make a good start. In other words, the processes of maturation have reached a certain stage, thanks to this supportive environment, which facilitated development. Then there was a failure of the environment, "which abruptly brought about a block in the process of maturation". A kind of recovery can take place, but a gap has opened in the child's line of life, from the child's own point of view.

> There has been an acute confusional state in the time-phase between the environmental failure and whatever there may be

in the way of a recovery. In so far as the child does not recover, the personality remains relatively disintegrated and the child is clinically restless and dependent on being directed by someone, or restrained by an institution.

(Winnicott, 1996: 216)

And we could add, we have seen how hope allows the development of antisocial behaviour as an appeal for help. Otherwise, the child who is without hope at the moment of deprivation, will become an adult incapable of developing an emotional relationship.

Deprivation is therefore a very different phenomenon from simple privation. Privation denotes maladjustment of the environment at the stage of absolute dependence. Deprivation occurs at the stage of relative dependence. The disruptions in the environment which modify the emotional development of a baby do not make for antisocial tendency. They generate personality distortion which leads to psychotic illness – he will suffer from psychiatric disorders or difficulty with the ordeal of reality or worse, which he can in fact sometimes manage. In this way, the antisocial tendency is inextricably linked to deprivation – which is, as we know, the loss of something that we have already possessed.

Delinquency, a sign of hope

In a letter to Clifford H. Scott of 19 March 1953, Winnicott again raises the subject of the difference that exists for him between the mad child and the asocial child, in the way that society treats them:

> The antisocial child, often a hopeless case, always gets attention, whereas the mad child finds it very difficult to get proper attention. Indeed madness is not recognized in childhood by society and treatment for the mad child is often lacking unless the child can turn round into being antisocial. Do you agree with this sort of statement?
>
> (Winnicott, 1999: 48)

He stresses once again that the antisocial act is a way of appealing to the environment, an attempt to recover what was lost. But to lose, one must have something to lose, so first there must be the establishment of basic security.

Delinquency is an appeal, an appeal for energetic measures to be taken, but not for vengeful retaliation. And if this appeal is not understood or dealt with in the family, then the child will turn to a wider circle – the extended family, school, society in general. In adolescence, extreme angst can lead to delinquency, as we will see in the chapter on adolescence. To understand this call for help, the adult must be aware of the hate that will be aroused in him by the behaviour of the antisocial child. He writes "It seems to me doubtful whether a human child as he develops is capable of tolerating the full extent of his own hate in a sentimental environment. He needs hate to hate" (Winnicott, 1992: 202).

In *Hate in the Counter-Transference*, a text written in 1947, Winnicott recounts how, just after the war, he and his wife had taken into their home a young antisocial boy.

> He was the most lovable and most maddening of children, often stark staring mad. But fortunately we knew what to expect. We dealt with the first phase by giving him complete freedom and a shilling whenever he went out. He had only to ring up and we fetched him from whatever police station had taken charge of him. [...] It was really a whole-time job for the two of us together.
>
> At crises I would take him by bodily strength, without anger or blame, and put him outside the front door, whatever the weather or the time of day or night. There was a special bell he could ring, and he knew that if he rang it he would be readmitted and no word said about the past. He used this bell as soon as he had recovered from his maniacal attack.
>
> The important thing is that each time, just as I put him outside the door, I told him something; I said that what had happened had made me hate him.

After the war, many of these wartime hostels were closed down. Some of them were maintained, and others created, and it was in these "peacetime hostels" where the therapeutic experiment continued. Winnicott's dedication during all these years, week after week, to working with the adults responsible for these living units, as well as the audience encountered in his broadcasts on the radio, led him to play an important role, together with Clare Britton, in the adoption of the 1948 Children's Act (laws protecting children in difficulty). He was one of the four psychoanalysts, together with John Bowlby, Susan Isaacs and Clare Britton, who were consulted by the Curtis Committee, which had been set up to reflect on these problems.

Towards the end of his life, Winnicott will claim that it is in its approach to the problem of the antisocial tendency that psychoanalytical findings will have been most effectively used.

Note

1 Letter to the *British Medical Journal*, 16 December 1939.

References

Dethiville, Laura. 2014. *Donald W. Winnicott: A New Approach*, London, Karnac Books.

Winnicott, Donald W. 1945a. "Home Again", in *Deprivation and Delinquency*, London, Routledge, or in *The Collected Works of D.W. Winnicott*, vol.2.

Winnicott, Donald W. 1945b. "The Return of the Evacuated Child", in *Deprivation and Delinquency*, London, Routledge, or in *The Collected Works of D.W. Winnicott*, vol. 2.

Winnicott, Donald W. 1947. "Residential Management as Treatment for Difficult Children", in *Deprivation and Delinquency*, London, Routledge, or in *The Collected Works of D.W. Winnicott*, vol. 3.

Winnicott, Donald W. 1953. "Symptom Tolerance in Paediatrics", in *Through Paediatrics to Psychoanalysis*, London, Karnac Books, or in *The Collected Works of D.W. Winnicott*, vol. 4.

Winnicott, Donald W. 1967. "D.W.W. on D.W.W.", in *Psycho-Analytic Explorations*, London, Karnac Books, or in *The Collected Works of D.W. Winnicott*, vol. 8.

Winnicott, Donald W. 1990. "Delinquency as a Sign of Hope", in *Home is Where We Start From*, London, Penguin Books, or in *The Collected Works of D.W. Winnicott*, vol. 8.

Winnicott, Donald W. 1992. "Hate in the Countertransference", in *Through Paediatrics to Psychoanalysis*, London, Karnac Books, or in *The Collected Works of D.W. Winnicott*, vol. 3.

Winnicott, Donald W. 1996. *Therapeutic Consultation in Child Psychiatry*, London, Karnac Books, or in *The Collected Works of D.W. Winnicott*, vol. 10.

Winnicott, Donald W. 1999. *The Spontaneous Gesture*, London, Karnac Books, or in *The Collected Works of D.W. Winnicott*, vol. 4.

Winnicott, Donald W. 2012. "The Antisocial Tendency", in *Deprivation and Delinquency*, London, Routledge, or in *The Collected Works of D.W. Winnicott*, vol. 5.

Chapter 6

Aggression and destructiveness

Here, we have to reverse our usual manner of proceeding if we want to approach Winnicott's theory of aggression. The orthodox theory has it that aggression is always a reaction to the encounter with the principle of reality, whereas in fact it is the impulse which creates the quality of the externalization. He writes in *Playing and Reality*: "There is no anger in the destruction of the object to which I am referring, though there could be said to be joy at the object's survival" (Winnicott, 1994: 86). In fact, initially we cannot speak of the infant's intentional aggression, and here again the issues of vocabulary are essential. Winnicott writes in *Aggression and its Relation to Emotional Development*, "confusion exists through our using the term aggression sometimes when we mean spontaneity" (Winnicott, 1992: 217), and here we find a small phrase which completely changes the way we read his developments on aggression. First, we must not forget that the word "aggression" comes from the Latin *agredior*, go towards, advance. I proposed in a previous book to translate this "go towards" by "modifying infringement".

Initially an instinctive motricity exists, which goes out to the world and lets the infant test his own body, a body which is at that moment his only language and his only means of communication.

Primary instinctive motricity

At this stage, there is no attack, no envy, nor aggression in the infant's movement. "It is no good saying that a baby of a few days old envies the breast", states Winnicott (1994: 124), criticizing the position of Melanie Klein. According to him, at this period of life it is "nothing else but living", pure motricity which already starts in prenatal life. It is the mother's interpretation of the infant's movement which will, *a posteriori*, take on an aggressive tone – an interpretation which the infant will register as such in his psyche. During her first interview, a mother once told me: "Anyway, he has always been like that, already in my tummy, he was kicking me."

At this early age, aggression *cannot be said* to be part of the infant's fantasy. If, for whatever reason, an infant at one point really hurts the mother, it can only be by accident. On the other hand, the adult will feel attacked and wounded. One mother he knew said:

> When the baby was brought to me she went for my breast in a savage way, tore at the nipples with her gums, and in a few moments blood was flowing. I felt torn to pieces and terrified. It took me a long time to recover from the hate roused in me against the little beast, and I think this was a big reason why she never developed real confidence about good food.
>
> (Winnicott, 1939/1964: 87)

The immature and dependent baby is overcome by impulsive excitement which can be felt as annihilation. At that moment, the environment must play the role of a guard against excitement and give meaning to a menacing experience (which Winnicott calls "primitive agonies"). To relieve the tension, the infant moves about, and cannot know that this movement is likely to hurt someone else unintentionally. So for the infant, the "going towards" is indistinguishable from a libidinal movement. Winnicott insists on the fact that it is a life-force which, coupled with instinctive tension, needs to find relief. Freud had already described the whole of this movement as a kind of vital aggressive instinct, which is the aggressive component of the libido and which can be regarded as a legacy of animal instinct.

In various different texts, Winnicott calls it "instinctive aggressiveness", "theoretical greed", "primary appetite-love", "mouth love". In one of his last texts, he writes that he could have called it "love-strife drive". This is a question which preoccupied him his whole life, and we can easily see from his work the time he took to clearly outline his ideas, faced with widely accepted theory. Furthermore, a long-lasting translation error could have us think that Winnicott imagined a baby which was possibly destructive. But for Winnicott, the baby is not *cruel*, as the translations persist in claiming. It is *ruthless*, an Old English that which means "without regard to others", "having no compassion". If there is any cruelty, at that moment it can only come from the adult. Winnicott evokes the *pre-ruth* stage, when the infant is of course without regard for the other, because for the baby, the other is not yet constituted as such and the baby has not yet defined for himself a me and a not-me. Incidentally, Winnicott, who can often be reproached for his way of writing, shows great precision in his vocabulary here. When he uses the words *cruel* or *cruelty*, it is always to describe the adult. The new-born baby is not "cruel", just as he does not know how to hate. There is nothing in the new-born baby of primary sadism, nor the possibility to express hate. Hate is a sophisticated feeling that implies a whole person, and the infant has not yet reached this stage.

This precision represents a crucial point and roundly criticizes the theory of Melanie Klein and her concept of the cruel infant. The many errors in the translation of this idea of *ruthlessness* have led to a misinterpretation of Winnicott's work and its perception of the very beginning of psychic life: for him, what comes is primary instinctual motility. He writes: "The essential principle is that by active adaptation to simple needs, the individuals can *be* and need not know of the environment" (Winnicott, 1990a: 130). At this point, hunger or colic can be felt like something as exterior as a clap of thunder. And it is the psychic stance of the mother which will set the tone of this merger. For, to this going towards, to this modifying attack, it is the other who will respond and give it meaning, the other who will react in a projective mode and from their own fantasies. If the mother can identify herself with the baby's needs and allow herself to be used in a living way, if she is able to offer her infant a instinctual satisfaction with the violence that sometimes accompanies it, she does not feel attacked. In other words, if she maintains her psychic *holding* during the experience, she allows the infant to live the experience without being destroyed. For the moment the appetite is satisfied, the desire disappears, and the infant has lost that which constituted it. He ends up alone and lost in a tasteless world. Winnicott writes:

> In the most primitive state, which may be retained in illness, and to which regression may occur, the object behaves according to magical laws, i.e. it exists when desired, it approaches when approached, it hurts when hurt. Lastly it vanishes when not wanted.
>
> This last is most terrifying and is the only true annihilation. To not want, as a result of satisfaction, is to annihilate the object. This is one reason why infants are not always happy and contented after a satisfactory feed.
>
> (Winnicott, 1945: 153)

The appetite will return, of course, but the *infans* does not know it yet. In the meantime, it is the permanence of the environment which guarantees the preservation of a global container which allows the child to have an experience of unity around his own sensory world. He/she has lost the mother he desired, but the familiar environment stays: the smell and contact of the breast, the comfort of being carried, the "sounds of the mother",[1] the eye contact. The traumatism of the instinctual demands followed by the traumatism of satisfaction have provoked a gap in the continuity of existence. The right care of an adequate environment has permitted a "restoration", in the Winnicott sense. After a brief failing, the object is still there, alive; that is, the same, destroyed for a short period of time, but alive once more. The work of detoxification (the sense Wilfred R. Bion gives to this term) has permitted the process to be lived in its entirety, in such a way that it is not fragmentary, but a source of enrichment. As Bion contends:

> A baby may not be in contact with the breast, but quite soon it can follow the mother about with the eyes. In this way it is possible to have a good relationship with the mother who isn't even in contact with the baby.
>
> (Bion, 1987: 114)

On the other hand, due to her very history, fragility, and the circumstances, the mother sees the movement of her baby towards the world, towards life, in a negative way. If she feels in danger, attacked, her manner of *holding* her baby will differ during this experience, however slight and restrained.

Faced with the traumatism due to the satisfaction of his need, in other words the loss of desire, the infant has no way out of the situation. "Mother may easily gratify an oral drive and by so doing violate the infant's ego function" (Winnicott, 1990b: 57). For the infant, the object has well and truly disappeared (for a short time, but he does not know it yet). He thinks he has destroyed it. This is the "destruction of the object". It is no longer there as an object to be desired, therefore it is no longer there at all. In the place of the loving mother there is a void. "There is a hole, where previously there was a full body of richness" (Winnicott, 1954–1955: 268), "since a source of zest for life has gone suddenly, and the infant does not know it will return" (Winnicott, 1954–1955: 268). The infant is himself transformed. He was overwhelmed by a sensation that was admittedly unpleasant, but which was his, which was part of his body experience, which was him. After the satisfaction of his need, this sensation will equally disappear.

Positive destructiveness

So the child is fooled by food! He feels the relief-pleasure of the end of his pulsional excitement, but at the same time he finds himself dispossessed of a feeling that was his. He is different; the mother is also different. For a short while he is confused (for he cannot yet link together the mother of phases of excitement and the mother of phases of calm). He thinks he has destroyed that which is indispensable to him and which is part of him, for we must not forget that at this moment he is part of his environment, an environment which is taken for granted. Suddenly, instead of this spontaneous drive – this modifying infringement – being considered as an accomplishment, a movement towards the other, there is a degree of inhibition, there is danger, which leads to a limitation in what Winnicott calls creativity.

In fact, Winnicott makes a distinction between "positive destruction" and "pathological destruction". Positive destruction is what we have just described, that which carries out the destruction of the object followed by its survival. This sequence presents the object as real, outside the realm of the baby's omnipotence. It is a vital process. He points out that real means "being part of the sphere of shared reality" and not just "beamed projections". The object is revealed as something that resists hypothetical destruction. It loses its status as subjective object. It becomes external, another subject. And he adds, from this point it can begin to be loved. Thus, to be able to love and tolerate being loved, it has to experience maximum destruction followed by the survival of the object. We are reminded that Winnicott refuses the term primary object, preferring the setting up of an average environment that allows the emerging young subject to grow up as close as possible to his potential.

The following is a very poetic dialogue he imagined taking place between the infant and the object.

> I find you.
> You survive what I do to you as I come to recognize you as not-me
> I use you.
> I forget you.

> But you remember me.
> I keep forgetting you;
> I lose you:
> I am sad.
>
> (Winnicott, 1987: 103)

This experience of destruction followed by the survival of the object marks the subject's access to *real* life, in direct contact with *real* objects, which can be loved to the extent that they can be destroyed in fantasy and survive in reality. In this way the baby can begin to differentiate between the object of fantasy, that which he has the illusion of destroying, and the external object; that is, the other subject. This experience permits the emerging young human being to place the object external to himself. Thus the *infans* can create a world that in fact was already there, waiting to be discovered. This is Winnicott's paradox: because it has survived, the object becomes real; but it is also because it is real that it survives.

From then on, the object can be *used*, which means that *because of its capacity to survive* it will be found and possibly used. Winnicott explains that he only uses the word "destruction" – a term that he is not really satisfied with (perhaps because the right word has not been found) – in order to show that this only becomes effective in the case of *failure of the object to survive*. It is never the modifying impingement which is the cause of the destruction, but the object itself in its capacity to survive. This breakthrough, which is surely the key point in his thinking, has often been misconstrued. The use of everyday terms, like "aggression", "destruction" or "survival", and the particular sense that he gives them has led once again to a misunderstanding.

From the child's point of view, the survival of the object means that the object remains the same, to be related to and used. The destruction of an object that survives, which has neither reacted nor disappeared, allows it to be used.

Pathological destruction

The very first, natural movement has at the start no destructive aim. For it to become so depends on what the object resembles. If the object is destroyed (that is to say, if it reacts, if it becomes different), the baby takes the reaction of the environment for the quality of his movement. Consequently since this happens in the very early period when the baby has not yet differentiated the me and not-me, it is the baby who feels destroyed and in danger of chaos and disintegration.

The experience, such as we have described, is at the origin of what he calls "pathological destruction", secondary, which has not found a psychic place where it can be transformed and integrated. In fact, this is the movement we mean when we use the term "destructiveness" in everyday speech. It remains split, disunited, wandering. It will either be repressed, which will lead to an inhibition of creativity, or possibly act against the other or against oneself. These phenomena are traditionally attributed to the death instinct. We are not going to redefine the death instinct according to Freud or Melanie Klein, but rather underline the points of divergence, keeping in mind that Winnicott was her supervisee, and it was a long time before he could rid himself of her influence. It was in 1920, in "Beyond the Pleasure Principle", that we first see Freud use the term "death instinct". We must remember that Freud never demanded his followers to adhere to this concept and this perspective: it was never a *shibboleth*. What we often forget is that several years later, Melanie Klein enhanced this Freudian idea her own way, and in today's analytic Tower of Babel, we need to be prudent and make it clear each time what we are referring to, when it is question of death instinct.

Freud, Melanie Klein and the death instinct

Melanie Klein believes that the death instinct is part of the biological equipment of the little human being. The same can apply to envy, hate and sadism, which she attributes to the child at the very beginning of life, thus fostering the image of a cruel, sadistic baby. The problem comes from the fact that she transformed a theory that Freud considered simply speculative (and which he himself took great precautions with) into a kind of dogma, a certitude that became the basis of her theory. We should remember that it is the Kleinian position regarding the death instinct which was at the centre of the famous "controversies" which shook the British Psychoanalytical School between 1941 and 1945.

Winnicott has always expressed his disagreement with Melanie Klein on this point. As we said, for him envy, sadism and hate cannot be inborn instinctual drivers. They develop in due course according to the primary environment that the child is part of at the beginning.

His theory is that the concept of the death instinct seems to disappear quite quickly, simply because it is no longer necessary. The aggression is seen rather as an evident sign of life.

What is more, in a rather caustic letter addressed to Hans Thorner on 17 March 1966, he writes:

> I hope you were pleased with the reception of your paper last night. It was very interesting and important. In regard to the tiny detail that I threw in at the end, this certainly did not call for a reply. I would like to say, however, that it is very confusing in the Society when various terms are used as if they were fully accepted. I am sure you know exactly what you mean when you say "dangerous parts … derivatives of the death instinct … must be expelled", etc, etc. I myself do not know what you mean and at least half the Society will feel that you are simply saying "death instinct" instead of using the words "aggression" and "hate". You may feel this is very unimportant, as indeed it is in the context of your paper, but it would be really valuable in the Society if we could find a common language. Sometime or other when you have nothing to do would you feel like rewriting that sentence without using the words "death instinct" just for my benefit? Thanking you again for the paper.
>
> (Winnicott, 1999: 154)

On no account does he deny "the clinically observed facts" which led Freud to the development of this concept of the death instinct. He implies another substructure. And he adds: "I have never been in love with the death instinct and it would give me happiness if I could relieve Freud of the burden of carrying it forever on his Atlas shoulders" (Winnicott, 1969: 242).

For him, the death instinct cannot be part of the instinctual apparatus of the little human being, but is a life instinct where, if the violence is not metabolized with the help of the human by his side, it can be experienced as annihilating and deadly. The immature psyche of the *infans* cannot integrate so much excitement *per se*. As we have seen, without the aid of an environment as a protective shield against excitement, the baby is caught up in what Winnicott calls "primitive agony", "a term which includes the word death".

In his article "L'enfant mal accueilli et sa pulsion de mort" (1929), Sándor Ferenczi asks the question in these terms. At the time of writing, and loyal to Freud, he cannot abandon the term "death instinct", but when he talks of those "patients who are suffering from a congenital weakness in their capacity to live" (Freud's term), he attributes this weakness to previously endured traumatisms, namely the influence of the environment.

In his excellent book *L'Ile des rêves de Sandor Ferenczi*, José Jiménez Avello introduces the term death passion to describe "the vestigial passion which the trace of the sadistic act of the other leaves in the subject". The corollary for the subject will be inoculation, like a "foreign transplant of this death passion, a profound imprint of suffering which disrupts the vital balance to the point of allowing it to merge with something constitutional and instinctual" (Avello, 2013: 100). In the notes written at the end of his life (Avello, 2013), Ferenczi will write: "Nothing but life instinct". This is what Winnicott develops.

Hate

The problem of hate arises because of these developments. We have seen that at the beginning, the infant is not equipped to feel love or hate. These are feelings that imply a personality which is already integrated. Moreover, we should stress that to speak of instinctive love or ruthless love does not help us understand.

> However early integration may be achieved – perhaps integration occurs earliest at the height of excitement or rage – there is a theoretical earlier stage in which whatever the infant does that hurts is not done in hate. I have used the term "ruthless love" in describing this stage.
>
> (Winnicott, 1991)

> it disturbed the continuity of his innate developmental processes before the psyche-soma had become sufficiently well organized to hate or to love. Instead of hating these environmental failures the individual became disorganized by them because the process existed prior to hating.
>
> (Winnicott, 1954)

There is no primary sadism in a child, and it is not possible for the child to feel hate. Freud wrote:

> We might at a pinch say of an instinct that it "loves" the objects after which it strives for purposes of satisfaction, but to say that it "hates" an object strikes us as odd, so we become aware that the attitudes of love and hate cannot be said to characterize the relation of instincts to their objects, but are reserved for the relations of the ego as a whole to objects.
>
> (Freud, 1968: 39)

For his part, Winnicott claims: "I suggest that the mother hates the baby before the baby hates the mother, and before the baby can know his mother hates him" (Winnicott, 1991: 200). The baby's need for his mother is ruthless, as we have seen, and that arouses in her short-lived movements of hate. In a famous text (Winnicott, 1991: 201) he lists with a touch of humour the reasons why a young mother might feel hate for her baby:

> The baby is a danger to her body in pregnancy and at birth.
> The baby is an interference with her private life, a challenge to preoccupation.
> To a greater or lesser extent a mother feels that her own mother demands a baby, so that her baby is produced to placate her mother.
> The baby hurts her nipples even by sucking, which is at first a chewing activity.
> He is ruthless, treats her as scum, an unpaid servant, a slave.
> She has to love him; excretions and all, at any rate at the beginning, till he has doubts about himself.
> He tries to hurt her, periodically bites her, all in love.
> He shows disillusionment about her.
> His excited love is cupboard love, so that having got what he wanted he throws her away like orange peel.
> The baby at first must dominate, he must be protected from coincidences, life must unfold at the baby's rate and all this needs his mother's continuous and detailed study.
> For instance, she must not be anxious when holding him, etc.
> At first he does not know at all what she does or what she sacrifices for him. Especially he cannot allow for her hate.
> He is suspicious, refuses her good food, and makes her doubt herself, but eats well with his aunt. [...]
> If she fails him at the start she knows he will pay her out for ever.

He excites her but frustrates – she mustn't eat him or trade in sex with him.

This declaration of Winnicott's is generally poorly received,[2] since nothing is more difficult to admit than the hate of a mother for her baby. It is an idea that is violently rejected, since it constitutes a very early defence mechanism, which disregards the hate that has been directed at us. The news items about infanticide or extreme child abuse – the subject of much media exposure today – allow us to continue believing that this murderous hate is only found in isolated monstrous individuals, and that it is not part of everyday life. And yet it is necessary to recognize this hate in order not to project it. Winnicott writes that

> a mother has to be able to tolerate hating her baby without doing anything about it. She cannot express it to him. If, for fear of what she may do, she cannot hate appropriately when hurt by her child, she must fall back on masochism, and I think it is this that gives rise to the false theory of a natural masochism in women.
> (Winnicott, 1991: 202)

This point of view could be called revolutionary, and it opens up many perspectives. Because who can a young mother talk to about her ambivalence towards her new-born baby? Certainly not to the father of her child; certainly not to her own mother since that would be acknowledging that she was not as good a mother; certainly not to her friends, who seem so happy in their successful motherhood. To talk of hate does not only undermine the indestructible myth of mother love, it is also an admission that there is real incompetence there. One of my patients, who was painfully blocked due to her personal history, was extremely alleviated after a session where these violent movements could be given a name and discussed. Afterwards the relationship with her child was significantly modified. And yet even a long time after this session, she still sometimes says "When I didn't love him", when she thinks back to that time.

In fact the mother has to be clear about her own hate to be able to receive the spontaneous movement of her child, this offensive impulse, without feeling herself attacked by hate (or what she feels it is) which would rebound on her by projective identification. The mother should be able to anticipate this hate so as not to be submerged by it. To deny hate leads to the establishment of "counter investment", which will mean too many distorted messages for a child who is directly connected to the emotional world of his mother. It is the language of gestures, the tone and rhythm of the voice, the seeking and rejecting of contact, and the comfortable or uncomfortable position which will be direct signifiers, since they all reveal the unconscious truth of the relationship that the mother builds at that moment. And we must bear in mind that they are only moments.

This hate, which is inherent to the primary environment, is always likely to be experienced by the child as being part of him or herself. Do we not often see in the clinic moments of auto-destruction, suicide attempts, failed lives, which we are tempted to call "the culture of the death instinct", whereas they are simply the enactment of a death wish resulting from internalized maternal or paternal objects? Margaret Little recounts how one day during her therapy Winnicott said: "Your mother, I hate her." This intervention is often misconstrued. It is definitely not a counter-transferential reaction by identification to his patient. What he meant was that he, as her analyst, would take that hate upon himself. Margaret Little adds that from that day on she ceased to put her life in danger by thoughtless behaviour.

One of my patients, in her third analysis, was struggling in a conflictual relationship with her mother and was accumulating destructive life choices. Her previous analysts had always interpreted the Oedipal situation that was still driving her to battle against her mother. None of them had succeeded in changing anything. From elements of her early childhood, we were able to reveal her mother's unconscious wish for her death. She was strengthened by this understanding of something she had always felt, and one day she asked her mother, with no aggressiveness or vindication: "Mummy, whatever happened between us?" Perhaps it was the calm nature of the question which brought the mother's reply: "I don't know, but I've always detested you." For my patient it was an incredible release. She had not dreamed it! She was now able to give meaning to many episodes in her life. She had finally survived and could leave the spiral of sorrow behind her.

Notes

1 An expression of Françoise Dolto.
2 His confirmation of the hate of the analyst for the patient is equally rejected. We will come to this later.

References

Avello, José Jiménez. 2013. *L'Ile des rêves de Sandor Ferenczi. "Rien que la pulsion de vie"*, Paris, Campagne Première.
Bion, Wilfred R. 1987. *Clinical Seminars and Four Papers*. London, Fleetwood Press.
Freud, Sigmund. 1968. "Pulsions et destins de pulsions", in *Métapsychologie*, Paris, Gallimard, coll. Folio essais.
Winnicott, Donald W. 1939/1964. "Aggression", in *Deprivation and Delinquency*, London, Routledge, or in *The Collected Works of D.W. Winnicott*, vol. 2.
Winnicott, Donald W. 1945. "Primitive Emotional Development", in *Through Paediatrics to Psychoanalysis*, London, Karnac Books, or in *The Collected Works of D.W. Winnicott*, vol. 2.
Winnicott, Donald W. 1954. "Mind and Its Relation to the Psyche-Soma", in *Through Paediatrics to Psychoanalysis*, London, Karnac Books, or in *The Collected Works of D.W. Winnicott*, vol. 3.
Winnicott, Donald W. 1954–1955. "The Depressive Position in Normal Emotional Development", in *Through Paediatrics to Psychoanalysis*, London, Karnac Books, or in *The Collected Works of D.W. Winnicott*, vol. 4.
Winnicott, Donald W. 1969. "The Use of an Object in the Context of *Moses and Monotheism*", in *Psycho-Analytic Explorations*, London, Karnac Books, or in *The Collected Works of D.W. Winnicott*, vol. 9.
Winnicott, Donald W. 1987. "Communication Between Infant and Mother, and Mother and Infant, Compared and Constrasted", in *Babies and Their Mothers*, London, Merloyd Lawrence, or in *The Collected Works of D.W. Winnicott*, vol. 8.
Winnicott, Donald W. 1990a. "The Earliest State", in *Human Nature*, London, Routledge, or in *The Collected Works of D.W. Winnicott*, vol. 11.
Winnicott, Donald W. 1990b. "Ego Integration in Child Development", in *The Maturational Process*, London, Karnac Books, or in *The Collected Works of D.W. Winnicott*, vol. 6.
Winnicott, Donald W. 1991. "Hate in the Countertransference", in *Through Paediatrics to Psychoanalysis*, London, Karnac Books, or in *The Collected Works of D.W. Winnicott*, vol. 3.
Winnicott, Donald W. 1992. "Aggression in Relation to Emotional Development", in *Through Paediatrics to Psychoanalysis*, London, Karnac Books, or in *The Collected Works of D.W. Winnicott*, vol. 3.
Winnicott, Donald W. 1994. "The Use of an Object and Relating through Identification", in *Playing and Reality*, London, Routledge, or in *The Collected Works of D.W. Winnicott*, vol. 8.
Winnicott, Donald W. 1999. *The Spontaneous Gesture*, London, Karnac Books, or in *The Collected Works of D.W. Winnicott*, vol. 4.

Chapter 7

Adolescence

We are always citing Winnicott's work concerning the new-born baby and its interrelation with its environment. However there is another period in life that Winnicott's writings help us with, and that is adolescence.

Winnicott had a highly personal and very modern approach to this subject, at a time when adolescent contestation was sweeping Europe – particularly in Britain, where there were serious problems with hooligans. He wrote two important texts on this question: the first, "Struggling through the Doldrums" in 1962; the second "Contemporary Concepts of Adolescent Development and their Implications for Higher Education" in 1968. The experience he acquired with children evacuated during the war was decisive in his method of dealing with this problem. After the war he continued to see an impressive number of adolescents, both in his private practice and at the hospital.

His common-sense approach was relatively optimistic. In fact his opinion was that the media were making too much of what were called "problem teenagers", and "Moreover, when a miracle happens, like the Beatles, there are those adults who wince when they could sigh a sigh of relief" (Winnicott, 1964: 157). His opinion, perhaps difficult to accept, was that in short, adults envy the teenagers and their infinite possibilities: "The big threat from the adolescent is the threat to the bit of ourselves that has not really had its adolescence. This bit of ourselves makes us resent these people being able to have their phase of the doldrums" (Winnicott, 2000: 155). Winnicott's own adolescence was ended too soon by the start of the First World War, which saw him lose many friends. And now the fathers of these problem teenagers are those whose infancy and adolescence suffered from the events of the Second World War. "It is indeed distressing for adults who have been themselves deprived of adolescence to watch boys and girls all round them in a state of florid adolescence" (Winnicott, 2000: 148). At the same time he adds:

> the adolescent striving that makes itself felt over the whole world today needs to be met, needs to be given reality by an act of confrontation. Confrontation must be personal. Adults are needed if adolescents are to have life and lifeness.
> (Winnicott, 1971)

Today we are witnessing an unmitigated fetishizing of adolescence. You must "get through adolescence", just as you need "time to mourn", or "must have a security blanket" as a child. What is more, we clearly see that children are pushed earlier and earlier into adolescence. How often do we hear in our interviews with parents the phrase "He/she is a really early adolescent"?[1] – where the apparently worried tone conceals a kind of pride most of the time. In fact the borderlines between teenagers and parents are increasingly undefined and today's parents often behave like adolescents – kidults, a word which describes this phenomenon very well. We live in a world where adolescence is the fashion, and this movement is orchestrated for marketing purposes.

If we refer to the etymology, "adolescence" comes from the Latin *adolescere*, which means "growing up", a definition that reminds us of how Winnicott stresses that the "time factor" is essential. In one of his humorous texts, "Youth Will Not Sleep" (Winnicott, 1968: 156), where he replies to an article in *The Times* on the hooligan phenomenon, he recalls a quotation from Shakespeare's *The Winter's Tale*: "I would there were no age between sixteen and three-and-twenty or that youth would sleep out the rest; for there is nothing in between but getting wenches with child, wronging the ancientry, stealing, fighting" (Winnicott, 1968).[2] In Shakespeare's time, the concept of adolescence did not exist. We went from childhood to adulthood (*adultus*: he who has finished growing up) passing over puberty. Shakespeare staged young adults with the modus operandi prevalent at the time, in particular the right to act instead of thinking.

When children come to adolescence, their parents can be driven to regress to their own adolescence, which reactivates unresolved psychic conflicts. The lifelong journey of the individual, driven by the process of maturation, passes through essential and structuring stages. We cannot forego them without some damage, and often the non-experience recurs. To "go through adolescence" at 40 or 50 does not have the same social consequences as it had at 18. The whole family can find itself in turmoil, especially if the children themselves are coming to adolescence. The parents imagine that they can relive a more successful adolescence than theirs had been. At the same time there is fear of being in the same position as their parents, and finding themselves in turn the object of the hate that they themselves had felt – consciously or not – for the adult world. So they try to avoid the issue. But Winnicott states that this is the "the worst thing to do to your child", and adds "If the child is to become adult, then this move is achieved over the dead body of an adult" (Winnicott, 1986: 158). To be in the wrong place, means letting your child down at a critical time. And he goes on to say that

> in terms of the game, or the life-game, you abdicate just as they come to killing you. Rebellion no longer makes sense, and the adolescent who wins too early is caught in his own trap, must turn dictator, and must stand up waiting to be killed – to be killed not by a new generation of his own children, but by siblings. Naturally, he seeks to control them.
> (Winnicott, 1986: 160)

This is what happens in *The Lord of the Flies*, which we have already evoked in Chapter 5 when we dealt with deprivation. Unfortunately, this kind of reasoning can also bring about ways of right to act that explain what happens in a non-fictional world; for example, the Khmer Rouge dictatorship in Cambodia. The leaders had to maintain a reign of terror in order to protect themselves from their own kind. Thus, as Winnicott further states, the parents should be forewarned: "You sowed a baby and you reaped a bomb. In fact this is always true but it does not always look like it" (Winnicott, 1971: 145) However the parents can rarely provide help. The best they can do is to survive, that is to say "survive intact, and without changing colour, without relinquishment of any important principle. This is not to say they may not themselves grow" (Winnicott, 1971: 145).

Immaturity and the doldrums

Winnicott considers adolescent immaturity as something positive: it is a valuable element in the adolescent scene. It is the moment when we find the most exciting features of creative thought, new and fresh feeling, ideas for new living ... Immaturity is an essential element of health at adolescence. There is only one cure for immaturity and that is the *passage of time* and the growth into maturity that time may bring.

Immaturity is a precious part of the adolescent scene. If the adults abdicate, the adolescent becomes prematurely, and by false process, adult. Advice to society could be: for the sake of adolescents, and of their immaturity, do not allow them to step up and attain a false maturity by handing over to them responsibility that is not yet theirs, even though they may fight for it.

(Winnicott, 1971: 146)

"Struggling through the Doldrums" was translated into French as "L'Adolescence". But word for word, it should be "*en bataillant à travers les eaux encalmées*". In English, this evokes the idea of a passage of time, a special time, not particularly *a period of* adolescence, but rather a *period for* adolescence, a time when we need to struggle, "struggle to find ourselves". As Winnicott contends: "Society needs to include this as a permanent feature and to tolerate it, ... *but not to cure it*. The question is, has our society the health to do this" (Winnicott, 2000: 153–154).

Winnicott was born in Plymouth and was a good sailor. The metaphor "doldrums" – a term used by sailors – describes the time and place on the globe where a vessel is sometimes immobilized due to the absence of any wind. In this dreaded situation, the navigators do not know where the wind will eventually come from, or even if it will come at all. However, in spite of the immobilization, there is some movement and swell.

Adolescence is both a period of evaluation and anticipation. It is not about the blues or depression, as is often said, but a space that is necessary and incompressible. The process can be neither accelerated nor slowed down. Time is the only remedy, but this is a solution that is no help to an adolescent in the throes of his or her despair (Winnicott, 2000). For a boy or girl going through adolescence, it is normal to muddle through, it is not an illness.

An adolescent at the moment of adolescence

Adolescents generally consider that life does not go fast enough, but at the same time they want it to slow down. As Winnicott constantly reminds us: what we see are "these disorders in patients who are at the puberty period of growth and who are adolescents in so far as they can be" (Winnicott, 1963b: 244). This time of life, which is essentially that of discovery, must be experienced: "Each individual is engaged in a living experience, a problem of existing, and of the establishment of an identity" (Winnicott, 2000: 145).

Therefore the position of the adult is essential, whether it be in the family itself or, in the case of failure, in a residential care home. One of my young patients spoke of his brother as having "adolescence" as if it were scarlet fever, for example. In both cases, there is nothing that can be done other than offer support and avoid complications. On the other hand, adolescence is not an illness, unless it could be called the last childhood disease. It is not about treating it, but allowing a deployment to take place without serious damage for the future. Therefore the question is: how can he or she find a psychic or material space, a space in-between, neither too close nor too far away, which allows this period to be dealt with without encountering too great a catastrophe?

Adolescence constitutes a moment for the reshuffling of infantile identities and offers a perspective towards new potentialities, potentialities which need to be faced and which define limits and choices. Julia Kristeva, in *Les Nouvelles Maladies de l'âme* (Kristeva, 1993), abandons the idea of a chronological framework to adolescence and considers it an open structure which we must remain attentive to. In this way, during the analysis of adults, we often come across phenomena that typically refer back to the adolescent process. Consequently in the cure we see passages re-enacted that resemble moments of crisis and modification, with all the implied suffering. As a result we understand why certain adults, or later the adolescents in the adults we listen to, try by all possible means not to get through this ordeal. They therefore "freeze" the evolving processes and their own potentialities, whereas at the same time they succeed perfectly in certain areas of their life. They have acquired a "false maturity", according to Winnicott, and this will not be without consequences.

Octave Mannoni once said: "Human beings who have not been through their adolescent crisis become silly adults."[3] I imagine he was referring to people who have lost their capacity to live their lives creatively. This brings us to the constant and persistent misunderstanding between the "time for adolescence" and the "crisis of adolescence".

The "time for adolescence" and the "crisis of adolescence"

The crisis indicates the moment when the illness situates itself between recovery and death, a change that is generally decisive for better or for worse. It is also possible that at this moment there will be a sudden aggravation of a chronic condition. So the crisis of adolescence can be interpreted in two ways. In the first sense, it is a critical moment (crisis) which will shape the future of the subject. It can also be the moment when the more or less latent neurosis or the failure of a primitive organization is revealed with a particular violence and/or urgency. This reminds me of those brilliant young students who fall apart during the years of preparatory classes, which is often a period of separation from their families, especially for those from the provinces.

In fact, each human being comes to adolescence with his own personal pattern, which depends on the way in which the essential stages of psychic structure have been traversed, as Winnicott sees it. The way has been fraught with difficulties, from the absolute dependence of the new-born until independence, through relative dependence; from the period of illusion to the establishment of "I am" and the phase of concern; from the infant-mother unit to the establishment of the transitional area; from spontaneous movement to the world of acceptance of maximum fantasmatic destruction, followed by the recreation of the world.

The way in which the environment permits the passage through these different stages defines this personal pattern with which each individual approaches the period of the Oedipus triangulation. Winnicott states: "The dynamic is the growth process, this being inherited by each individual. Taken for granted, here, is the good-enough facilitating environments ... nothing takes place in emotional growth except in relation to the environmental provision" (Winnicott, 1971: 139).

New wine into goat skin bottles

The hormonal changes in puberty bring about a reactivation of the experiences of the *infans*, and then of the child, a reactivation of the inherent conflicts at the complex moments he or she has lived through. Winnicott wonders how this ego organization deals with this new id advance? It is as if we put "new wine into goat skin bottles", he writes, and the new fermentation risks the explosion of everything. If we remember that the *infans* was completely helpless in face of a instinctual experience which he interpreted as foreign and persecuting and which seemed as exterior as "a hit or a clap of thunder", we can also equally understand that the adolescent feels helpless and in great distress in face of an instinctual experience which submerges him or her. The ego-coverage of the mother allowed the baby to integrate his experience in a way which did not annihilate him. In the same way, the problems that arise at puberty are identical to those of the early stages of life, when these same children were relatively inoffensive new-born babies or toddlers. But the game has changed and the possibilities of action are not the same.

In consultations at the *Centre medico-psycho-pédagogique* (CMPP), it is not unusual to interview adolescents whose family had already brought them to consultation as a small child. Often these first interviews had not led to psychotherapeutic treatment, for various reasons: a sudden improvement in the symptoms (flight into health), lack of availability, inadequate involvement by the parents, etc. When we study the case file, we find the same symptoms as in childhood, although the violence of a 17-year-old has greater implications that that of a three-year-old. We find equally unchanged (because nothing was ever done) the initial problems of the family constellation, which has suddenly had its defensive position weakened by the brutal arrival at adolescence of a family member.

Adolescence is also the moment when the child goes from infantile sexuality to genital sexuality; that is to say, the abandon of infantile sexual theories in favour of the reality of the sexual act and the pleasure it represents. It is sometimes at this very moment that certain events in early childhood will become clear. To discharge sexual tension the adolescent often turns to masturbation or to compulsive sex with another. And the access which is now possible to adult sexuality poses the question of the sexual object choice and gender identity.

For Winnicott, this phase is that of "sex prior to readiness for sex", that is to say immature sexuality, the encounter of two genitalia but not "two whole human beings, two subjectivities" (Winnicott, 2000).

On another level, the newfound physical strength of the adolescent boy or girl, the possibility they have of being able to talk and act, can precipitate destructive or auto-destructive behaviour. Growing up means taking the place of a parent. In unconscious fantasy, this is by nature an aggressive act. But now the physical strength of the adolescent increases the possibility of a violent act, either to another or to oneself. Winnicott warns us without undue sentimentality: "Let me choose to pick out one thing for special mention. *There will be suicides*" (Winnicott, 1963b: 245), because "how shall each one deal with something that really is new: the power to destroy and even to kill, a power which did not complicate the feelings of hatred that were experienced at the toddler age" (Winnicott, 2000: 146).

The issue of the feeling of existing in adolescence gives rise to the problem of separation and exile on which individuality is based. It is about an individual journey. And to be able to unfold this journey the way needs to be paved with adult markers. "The situation lacks its full richness if there is a too easy and successful avoidance of the clash of arms" (Winnicott, 1971: 145). There needs to be a confrontation – but confrontation is not a battle! Winnicott (1971: 147) explains: "The word 'confrontation' is used here to mean that a grown-up person stands up and claims the right to have a personal point of view, one that may have the backing of other grown-up people." As we have seen at the beginning of this chapter, it is not about "treating" an adolescent crisis. He adds: "We must not try to cure adolescents as if they were suffering from a psychiatric disorder" (Winnicott, 1963b: 244). And in "Psychotherapeutic Interview with an Adolescent", Winnicott states that there is nothing more difficult than having to "decide whether one is seeing a healthy boy or girl who is in the throes of adolescence or a person who happens to be ill, psychiatrically speaking, in the puberty age" (Winnicott, 1964: 326). For his part Octave Mannoni makes it clear that we don't know if some adolescent crises are the onset of mental illness, or whether the crises become mental illness because they have been hindered (Mannoni, 1984).

In *Deprivation and Delinquency*, Winnicott insists on the fact that:

> there exists only one real cure for adolescence: maturation. This and the passage of time do, in the end, result in the emergence of the adult person. The process cannot be hurried up, though indeed it can be broken into and destroyed by clumsy handling, or it can wither up from within when there is psychiatric illness in the individual.
>
> (Winnicott, 2000: 145)

So it is not about cure but support. This is something that must be borne in mind when working with adolescents. It represents an enormous amount of work for the therapist engaged in this kind of support. With an adolescent, the transference often reactivates psychic positions which had not necessarily been taken into account (I refer here to the remarkable work of De Silvestris, 2013). So to take on the role of the adolescent boy or girl in an unresolved combat with the parents and to find oneself in the position of an accomplice, or even instigator, in an imaginary battle represents a grave danger. This is particularly true if what we call the "adolescent paranoia" encounters objective support from the analyst. There could be a real risk of tipping over the edge into an authentic delirium and an attitude justifying this feeling of persecution, by the intervention of the entourage.

Just as dangerous is the identification of the analyst to a parental figure – which was Freud's mistake with the "young homosexual woman" or with Dora (Freud, 1954). We know what happened: both of them fled. In her old age, the "young homosexual woman" revealed that she attended the sessions because it was an occasion for her to meet her "lady friend", and she gave Freud exactly the answers he expected, even inventing the dreams she described. She had thus got even with her father (who had instigated the therapy), reassured Freud, who carried on the treatment, and was able to happily go and see her "lady friend". And at the age of 94 she continued to be scandalized by Freud's "smutty" interpretations (Rieder and Voigt, 2003).

In fact, although the adolescent is interested by psychoanalytical theories, he or she generally mistrusts psychoanalysis. The adolescent *doesn't want* to be understood. He or she has no wish for someone to explicitly underline the paradox of their behaviour and give an explanation for it. They fear that psychoanalysis will reveal their intimate thoughts and dread what is felt as a real psychic violation. They cannot tolerate someone tampering with the imaginary explanatory construction which they have built up around themselves. And most of all, they need to find opposite them an adult who will not fall into their many traps. They have the right to be unreasonable, ungrateful in face of someone who might be susceptible to survive by indicating he is not dupe.

The adolescent is an isolate

There is a strong incentive to consider adolescence as a kind of "psychic fallow period", a time without "form". For, as Winnicott writes,

"There is not yet a capacity to identify with parent figures without loss of personal identity" (Winnicott, 1963: 244) – a situation which could be summed up as: better nothing than betray the self. To a certain extent, the analyst is a go-between. "The analyst of an adolescent must expect to be tested out fully and must be prepared to use communication of indirect kind, and to recognize simple non-communication" (Winnicott, 1963a: 190). The period of adolescence repeats a phase of infancy – as we have already discussed. Essentially the adolescent is an isolate (just as the infant is an isolate), even if he/she goes around in a group, which Winnicott calls "a collection of isolates". "They can be seen to be forming groups on the basis of minor uniformities, and on the basis of some sort of group appearance which belongs to locality and age" (Winnicott, 2000).

> This preservation of personal isolation is part of the search for identity, and for the establishment of a personal technique for communicating which does not lead to violation of the central self. [...] At adolescence when the individual is undergoing pubertal changes and is not quite ready to become one of the adult community, there is a strengthening of the defences against being found. That which is truly personal and which feels real must be defended at all cost, and even if this means a temporary blindness to the value of compromise.
> (Winnicott, 1963a: 190)

Here again we find his main thesis, that of *the existential isolation of the individual.* One of the recurring problems of the adolescent lies in the fear of what he feels is submission to an adult way of life which, for the time being, he/she is rejecting, since adult life is not really tempting. Up to now, he/she has not had the opportunity to learn the difference between compromise and compromising. And in fact, by their behaviour, adolescents test the psychopathology of the adult. The so-called "crisis" is as much that of the adult as of the adolescent and, with luck, the adult may also come through it "modified".

Curiously enough, on several occasions Winnicott describes adolescent needs and compares them to those of the new-born baby. His theory is that the adolescent refuses "the false solutions", "which leads them to do certain things which are only too real from the point of view of society". So it is possible to gather together a list of what we may think are some of the needs of adolescents:

- the need to avoid the false solution: the need to feel real or to tolerate not feeling at all;
- the need to defy – in a setting in which their dependence is met and can be relied on to be met;
- the need repeatedly to prod society so that society's antagonism is manifest, and can be met with antagonism.

He goes on to say that adolescents play at being, and it is indispensable to allow them this liberty to play, for playing is important during this phase of the introduction of cross-identification, which is also a phase of undefined sex. In this regard, "to dress as" and "play" are almost "justified cross-dressing", and here lies the importance of *playing* in the transitional space. This outside space serves to create a distance, to avoid direct contact with reality. The adolescent's analyst must recognize this space and allow it to exist. Winnicott insists a great deal on "the therapy of life" which is the game at this moment. It is of capital importance that the family and society tolerate what happens during this passage, even if, as we can imagine, it will be difficult to accept at the family table individuals we have trouble in recognizing.

To play is to dream, and to dream is to live – this could be Winnicott's motto. Dreaming and living are of the same order. Just like the new-born baby, adolescents must at times see themselves as the creator of their world. Through disidentification-identification, and after many setbacks, the adolescent will be able to discover him/herself, thus avoiding a false solution.

And Winnicott adds further:

> This means that in the group that the adolescent finds to identify with, the extreme members of the group are acting for the total group. The identification to this act will make them feel real. Each will be loyal and will support the individual who will act for the group, although not one of them would have approved the thing that the extreme antisocial did.
>
> I think that this principle applies to the use of other kinds of illness. The suicide attempt of one of the members is very important to all the others. Or, one of them cannot get up, he is paralysed with depression, and has got a record-player playing very doleful music; he locks himself in his room and nobody can get near. The others all know this is happening, and every now and again he comes out and they have a bottle party or

something, and this may go on all night or for two or three days. Such happenings belong to the whole group and the group is shifting and the individuals are changing their groups, but somehow the individual members of the group use the extremes to help themselves *to feel real*, in their struggle to get through this doldrums period.

(Winnicott, 1991: 87)

Adolescence and delinquency

The problem of delinquency in adolescence brings us back to what we had found concerning the antisocial tendency. Winnicott asserts that antisocial behaviour is an SOS.

By the time the boy or girl has become hardened because of the failure of the communication, the antisocial act not being recognized as something that contains an SOS, and when secondary gains have become important, and great skill has been achieved in some antisocial activity, the nit is much more difficult to see, the SOS that is a signal of hope in the boy or girl who is antisocial.

(Winnicott, 1990: 90)

Delinquency is a clear sign of hope, a call for help. With a touch of humour, he states that it is easy to think like that when it is not your bicycle that has been stolen or your backside that has been kicked! And he repeats that what is necessary at that moment is not therapy but recuperation of the environmental provision that has been lost. He also insists on the necessity for places to exist like the wartime hostels, which were therapeutic in themselves. He writes about one of such hotels thus:

Rather quickly I learned that the therapy was being done in the institution by the walls and the roof; by the glass conservatory which provided a target for bricks, by the absurdly large baths for which an enormous amount of precious wartime coal had to be used up if the water was to reach up to the navel of the swimmers.

The therapy was being done by the cook, by the regularity of the arrival of food on the table, by the warm enough and perhaps warmly coloured bedspreads [...] Of course the boys ran away, they stole from the houses in the neighbourhood, and they kept breaking glass.

The sound of breaking glass took on epidemic proportions. Fortunately the champagne rhubarb was a long way away, towards the west, where exhausted members of staff could stand in the quiet and watch the sunset.

(Winnicott, 1970: 221)

We often criticize young people for making too much noise. In fact it is only true for a few of them. We are forgetting all those who suffer adolescence in silence. They keep their malaise to themselves and struggle through the doldrums alone or hang out with others, lying on the bed listening to music or stuck in front of their computer screen.

Many psychoanalysts today are addressing the issue of the "new pathologies" of addiction to virtual games. For 95 per cent of teenagers these addictions will last until the end of their adolescence. They are a way of waiting until the doldrums end, which is effective – and reassuring for the parents at first – but can, however, lead to a real addiction in certain cases. The proportion of pathological use is fairly low, but the phenomenon calls for the utmost caution.

Adolescence implies growing up, which takes time. While this is being accomplished, the parental figures must assume their changing responsibility.

The enormous success of the *Harry Potter* saga is partly due to its illustration of adolescent problems. In fact *Harry Potter* is the account of a long journey. Of course the principal combat is to avoid becoming a "Muggle" (that is, an adult who has no longer access to magic). The theme can be summed up as how to preserve the magic of childhood and become adult without compromising. The story starts when Harry Potter is 11 and ends when, at the age of 17, he has overcome numerous pitfalls and is able to live fully fledged love. In the meantime, he will have grown up in an ideal, magic place, containing and protective, the Hogwarts school. During the combat, he will have lost many loved ones who were so much part of him, he will have been confronted by a maximum of destructivity and his own destruction, in the strange game of cross-identification with Voldemort, the absolute evil. For this deprived child, who had lost a loving mother and father before the age of two, the antisocial tendency represented what we might call the leaven of a "non-compliance", a non-submission, intransigent and uncompromising. In the end, he had to lose the protection of the containing Hogwarts school, face the death of his childhood self and dare to love to be able to cross the bridge (see Dethiville, 2005: 105).

Notes

1 It is true to say that there is a real phenomenon of increasingly early puberty, which remains largely unexplained.
2 This line was in fact misquoted in both The *Times* and New Society. All the Shakespeare folios give "between ten and three and twenty" showing a closer correspondance than Winnicott had credited.
3 Personal communication.

References

De Silvestris, Pia. 2013. *Fragile Identité*, Paris, Campagne Première.
Dethiville, Laura. 2005. "Winnicott aurait-t-il joué au Sims?" in De l'âge de raison à l'adolescence: quelles turbulences à découvrir?, Toulouse, Erès.
Freud, Sigmund. 1954. "Fragment d'une analyse d'hystérie", in *Cinq Psychanalyses*, Paris, PUF.
Kristeva, Julia. 1993. *Les Nouvelles Maladies de l'âme*, Paris, Fayard.
Mannoni, Octave. 1984. "L'adolescence, est-elle analysable?", in *La Crise de l'adolescence*, Paris, Denoël.
Rieder, Inès and Voigt, Diana. 2003. *Sidonie Czillag. Homosexuelle chez Freud, lesbienne dans le siècle*, Paris, Epel.
Winnicott, Donald W. 1963a. "Communicating and Not Communicating, Leading to a Study of Certain Opposites", in *The Maturational Processes and the Facilitating Environment*, London, Routledge, or in *The Collected Works of D.W. Winnicott*, vol. 6.
Winnicott, Donald W. 1963b. "Hospital Care Supplementing Intensive Psychotherapy in Adolescence", in *The Maturational Processes and the Facilitating Environment*, London, Routledge, or in *The Collected Works of D.W. Winnicott*, vol. 6.
Winnicott, Donald W. 1964. "Psychotherapeutic Interview with an Adolescent", in *Psycho-Analytic Explorations*, London, Karnac Books, or in *The Collected Works of D.W. Winnicott*, vol. 7.
Winnicott, Donald W. 1968. "Youth Will Not Sleep", in *Deprivation and Delinquency*, London, Routledge, or in *The Collected Works of D.W. Winnicott*, vol. 7.
Winnicott, Donald W. 1970. "Residential Care as Therapy", in *Deprivation and Delinquency*, London, Routledge, or in *The Collected Works of D.W. Winnicott*, vol. 9.

Winnicott, Donald W. 1971. "Contemporary Concepts of Adolescent Development and their Implications for Higher Education", in *Playing and Reality*, London, Routledge, or in *The Collected Works of D.W. Winnicott*, vol. 9.

Winnicott, Donald W. 1986. "Adolescent Immaturity", in *Home is Where We Start From*, London, Penguin Books.

Winnicott, Donald W. 1990. "Delinquency as a Sign of Hope", in *Home is Where We Start From*, London, Penguin Books, or in *The Collected Works of D.W. Winnicott*, vol. 8.

Winnicott, Donald W. 1991. "Adolescence, Struggling through the Doldrums", in *The Family and Individual Development*, London, Brunner-Routledge, or in *The Collected Works of D.W. Winnicott*, vol. 6.

Winnicott, Donald W. 2000. "Struggling through the Doldrums", in *Deprivation and Delinquency*, London, or in *The Collected Works of D.W. Winnicott*, vol. 6.

Chapter 8

Regression

In analytical circles, regression has generally a rather poor reputation. Traditionally, the term implies "the return of the subject to the previous stages of his development" (Laplanche and Pontalis, 1967) It is therefore a step backwards that represents resistance, a defence mechanism and, more specifically, the action of the compulsion for repetition. For Freud, it was a negative episode in the cure which blocked the course of the analytical process, based on the verbalization and interpretation of the movements of the transference.

On the other hand, for Sándor Ferenczi, regression was a dynamic process. He thought that no analysis can be considered satisfactory unless a re-experiencing of the primitive trauma which is responsible for the formation of the personality and symptoms can be achieved. He therefore was convinced that more often than not the revivication in deep regression and trance permitted the resolution of splitting that had occurred following a trauma. In fact, during the initial experience, the feeling had been denied and disassociated. The objective was therefore that the subject might recognize that which he had experienced and re-establish the link with the affect felt at that time. For him, this form of regression was therapeutic. The role of the analyst was to accept it when it appeared, not to obstruct it and even sometimes to activate it. For when the analysis does not progress, it is always the fault of the analyst. Freud did not agree with certain aspects of this technique. Therapeutic regression later acquired a bad reputation and was gradually neglected.

It was Michael Balint who established the difference between benign and malignant regression, and Winnicott who pointed out the importance of regression in clinical work. As always, it is the clinical experience that leads him to take this mechanism into account whereas, as he wrote in connection with a case, he would have preferred to avoid it:

> I have therefore had a unique experience even for an analyst. I cannot help being different from what I was before this analysis started. Non-analysts would not know the tremendous amount that this kind of experience of *one* patient can teach, but amongst analysts can expect it to be fully understood that this one experience that I have had has tested psychoanalysis in a special way, and has taught me a great deal.
>
> The treatment and management of this case has called on everything that I possess as a human being, as a psycho-analyst, and as a paediatrician. I have had to make personal growth in the course of this treatment which was painful and which I would gladly have avoided. In particular I have had to learn to examine my own technique whenever difficulties arose, and it has always turned out in the dozen or so resistance phases that the cause was in a countertransference phenomenon which necessitated further self-analysis in the analyst.
>
> (Winnicott, 1954a: 280)

Briefly, I have had a patient (a woman now in middle age) who had had an ordinary good analysis before coming to me but who obviously still needed help. This case had originally presented itself as one in the first category of my classification, but although the diagnosis of psychosis would never have been made by a psychiatrist, an analytical diagnosis needed to be made that took into account a very early development of a false self. For treatment to be effectual, there had to be a regression in search of the true self. Fortunately in this case I was able to manage the whole regression myself, that is to say, without the help of an institution. I decided at the start that the regression must be allowed its head, and no attempt, except once near the beginning, was made to interfere with the regressive process which followed its own course. (The one occasion was an interpretation I made, arising out of the material, of oral erotism and sadism in the transference. This was correct but about six years too early because I did not yet fully believe in the regression. For my own sake I had to test the effect of one ordinary interpretation. When the right time came for this interpretation it had become unnecessary.) It was a matter of about three or four years before the depth of the regression was reached, following which there started up a progress in emotional development. There has been no new regression. There has been an absence of chaos, though chaos has always threatened.

(Winnicott, 1954a: 280)

So what does Winnicott mean by regression?

Regression according to Winnicott

Regression is the reverse of progress; that is, the reverse of the human being's natural movement, which tends to go towards the integration of psyche-soma and independence. This progress is usually borne by the process of maturity. This process starts at birth, is never totally complete and continues to strengthen in later childhood, in adulthood and even in old age. Inversely, regression is a return to early dependence, which requires an environment capable of meeting the situation of need. He emphasizes clearly that it is "regression to dependence and not specifically regression in terms of erotogenic zones" (Winnicott, 1954a: 281).

This movement is a manner of returning to the original situation of failure, a return to the most archaic period of existence. As we have seen in the preceding chapters, certain failures in the early environment of the infant have had the effect of blocking, or jamming a pathogenic situation. The subject defends himself by freezing the situation. However, there is unconscious hope that there will continue to be an opportunity for the unfreezing of this failure situation, so that it can be re-experienced positively during the regression.

So regression is not only the reverse of progress, it also demonstrates an efficient organization of the ego against the danger of annihilation. He states that:

> It is normal and healthy for the individual to be able to defend the self against specific environmental failure by a freezing of the failure situation. Along with this goes an unconscious assumption (which can become a conscious hope) that opportunity will occur at a later date for a renewed experience in which the failure situation will be able to be unfrozen and re-experienced.
>
> (Winnicott, 1954a: 281)

Note that the same vocabulary is also used by Jacques Lacan in the workshop entitled "L'acte analytique". He also used the term "freezing": "When there is not an appropriate environment in the first days and months of a baby's life, something can happen to cause this freezing" (Lacan, 1967–1968). He goes on to evoke the psychotic consequences of this situation. But the reconciliation of these two ways of seeing things stops here, since Lacan immediately castigates Winnicott for his concept of the false self, and he will always be against the use of regression in the cure.

One of my patients, at a certain moment at the start of this process, had dreamed that he was defrosting a refrigerator! So we find that every patient has a latent capacity to regress, which is usually proof of the ability of the patient to cure him or herself. It is normal and healthy for an individual to be able to freeze a situation awaiting a possibility of regression, instead of succumbing to chaos. For the sake of clarity, we can say that Winnicott refers here to the "false-self structures" – defensive structures that take on prematurely the function of "nursing by the mother, so that the infant or child adapts to the environment while at the same time protecting and hiding the true self" (Winnicott, 1989b: 43). These structures protect from psychosis and disintegration. So regression is expected after there has been a freezing of the failure situation, but it can only exist if the environmental conditions are adequate. Here we find something of what happens with the antisocial tendency.

Winnicott specifies that we must be very careful not to fall into the current trap of using the term "regression" indiscriminately. For example, he believes that it makes no sense to use the word regression to qualify infantile behaviour. "When we speak of regression in psycho-analysis we imply the existence of an ego organization and a threat of chaos" (Winnicott, 1954a: 281).

The beginning of his article "Metapsychological and Clinical Aspects of Regression Within the Psycho-Analytical Set-Up", he applies a fairly arbitrary distinction between three different categories of cases, "according to the technical equipment they require of the analyst". In the first group, he places the neurotic patients (who operate as whole persons), whose difficulties belong to the kind of psychoanalysis developed by Freud at the beginning of the twentieth century. In the second group, he places the patients who have not been able to achieve the stage of concern. The essential point in this case lies with the analyst and his capacity to survive. In the third group he places the patients whose analyses must address the early stages of emotional development. For these patients it is more a case of management. It is in this category that we find patients who need regression – a need to regress which at the same time as it characterizes the personal structure, has the value of communication: it represents a sign for the analyst of what is expected of him. For in this kind of situation, it is not just a question of satisfying or frustrating desires, but of meeting the need. He writes:

> If a regressed patient *needs* quiet, then without it nothing can be done at all. If the need is not met the result is not anger, only a reproduction of the environmental failure situation which stopped the process of self-growth.
> (Winnicott, 1954a: 288)

Above all, the patient must be able to count on the reliability of the analyst. A phrase of Winnicott's that described the position of the analyst in such moments of certain cures has been misused and wrongly interpreted. He never said that the analyst *should be* the mother in the transference. He developed the idea that in these particular phases "for a moment or for an hour or over a long period of time", the analyst finds himself "in a similar position to that of a mother and her newborn baby", due to the massive dependence of the patient. He highlights a parallel and not an equivalent. The analyst is *not* the mother in the transference, he fulfils a function. And like the mother of the *infans*, he must be clear about the feelings aroused in him by the objective behaviour of the patient, including his hate. This is the only way to understand when Winnicott says that it is indispensable for this type of patient to be able to "get a little bit of the real analyst". This is also how we come to the important idea of active adaptation that Winnicott elicits.

Winnicott maintained his whole life that in the case of serious pathologies, the reliability of the frame – the analyst being part of this frame – was more important that the interpretations. I would add at this point that Winnicott is careful to make a difference between *frame*, *setting* and *holding*.

Frame, setting and holding

The frame is established between the analyst and the patient, namely the timetable and frequency of the sessions, the amount of the fee, a prearrangement concerning holiday periods and missed sessions. The setting encompasses the analytic situation in its entirety, including the subjective aspects of the relationship, silent and non-verbal communication, how to formulate the interventions and handle the transference. The holding defines the way in which the analyst "contains" the situation reliably. It is this difference that inspires Winnicott to compare the work of the analyst during periods of regression to the mother's holding of her new-born baby. For it is not enough to listen. It's about taking it upon oneself, to transform and restore the material in a way the patient can integrate it. The analyst must be able to put into words the profound anxiety of that patient. It is about providing ego coverage. (Bion's personal vocabulary mentions the analyst's "apparatus for thinking": just as the "alpha-element" of the apparatus for thinking of the mother metabolizes the experience of the infant and gives it meaning, the work of the analyst consists of giving meaning and words to what he perceives is happening for his patient.)

The need to regress is not something we would wish on everyone, declares Winnicott. For it is not easy to succumb to regression, it takes a great deal of courage. "It is, one can well understand, very painful to the patient to be dependent unless one is actually an infant, and the risks that have to be taken in regression to dependence are very great indeed" (Winnicott, 1963b: 240). To let oneself go, take the risk of a regression – that is to say to have complete confidence in another – is a painful process and can be seen as extremely dangerous. For example, Winnicott recalls the case of a woman patient who saw herself in a dream as a tortoise with a soft shell, and this just before he was going away for a time. In her dream, she killed the tortoise to avoid suffering. Winnicott writes:

> This was herself and indicated a suicide tendency, and it was to cure this tendency that she had come for treatment. [...] My going away re-enacted a traumatic episode or series of episodes of her own babyhood. It was in one language as if I were holding her and then became preoccupied with some other matter so that she felt *annihilated*.
>
> (Winnicott, 1963a: 249)

It seems likely that by killing herself she would be taking control of the annihilation that was threatening her, due to the departure of her analyst. And incidentally this patient fell seriously ill at that moment, but without the cause of this illness ever being elucidated. Winnicott recalls: "Before I went I just had time, but just only, to enable her to feel a connection between the physical reaction and my going away" (Winnicott, 1963a: 249).

And what is more, she was a patient who had already experienced a long, classic analysis before that, and who very quickly (almost prematurely, says Winnicott) entered into a "regression to dependence" with him. He admits having made a mistake in starting this analysis just before undertaking a long-envisaged trip, which only goes to confirm his idea that the regression was waiting for the adequate environment to begin. He goes on to say that this case "might show the danger of underestimating transference dependence" (Winnicott, 1963a: 334), for as soon as we are dependent on someone, we are in danger. And what is more, in such cases the analyst cannot not avoid asking himself the reasons why a patient would prefer to kill themselves rather than live with the danger of annihilation.

Another clinical and theoretical aspect can be illustrated thus: when regression is prevented for some reason, we often witness breakdown accompanied by misidentified illness. Sometimes there are patients who absolutely need to regress but are not able to, due to a particular attitude of their analyst, on the grounds of a demanding external reality. In such cases, it is not rare to see them develop a psychosomatic illness, one of such auto-immune disorders that doctors do not know how to treat. At least a psychosomatic illness offers the opportunity of a *partial* regression in an environment which tries to adapt to the primary needs. However, Winnicott reminds us that this situation "which produces the much needed nursing, but not the insight or the mental care that can really make a difference" (Winnicott, 1963a: 253). So psychosomatic collapse represents a false solution, since it will not have a true structuring effect unless there is, on the part of the analyst, comprehension (in the sense of pulling together) and put into symbolizing words.

The reliability of the analyst

So the choice of regression is not down to the analyst! Here it is important to set the record straight, since in his own words "They say: Winnicott likes to regress his patients!" No, Winnicott did not like to regress his patients. He found it exhausting. Each regression demanded a great deal of time and availability. Moreover, in his "classic" schedule, he could only allow for one patient at a time to undertake the experience of deep regression (according to Margaret

Little, anyway). That being said, after his 1954 conference on "Aspects of Regression in the Analytic Set-Up", he accepted more and more patients in this category, referred to him by his colleagues. Just as it was for Ferenczi earlier, a large number of patients considered unanalysable, and in need of regression, were entrusted to him.

When regression occurs, it's up to the patient to bear it.

> In other words it would be pleasant if we were to be able to take for analysis only those patients whose mothers at the very start and also in the first months had been able to provide good-enough conditions. But this era of psychoanalysis is steadily drawing to a close.
>
> (Winnicott, 1954a: 291)

The minimum that a patient can expect from the analyst he/she is in analysis with is that he will not impede a regression he considers necessary and that he will be able to accompany it. Winnicott recounts the story of a woman patient whose analyst said to her: "Now, sit up, straighten up and speak!" Some may think that such an attitude was most healthy, for the analyst had made things clear and the patient knew *what she could not expect from him*, basically. She took leave of the analyst on good terms.

Furthermore, the danger does not lie in the regression but in the fact that the analyst is not ready to face this return to the past and the dependence which accompanies it. "It takes a great deal of courage to have a breakdown, but it may be that the alternative is *a flight to sanity*, a condition comparable to the manic defence against depression" (Winnicott, 1954a: 287).

In the work of Françoise Dolto, we find a similar theoretical approach to this idea of regression. The great French psychoanalyst recounts that it was after reading Freud that she developed the idea of an eventual regression by the subject to a much earlier bodily and sensorial experience during his/her adult life, particularly during the cure. Bearing this in mind, she studied how regression could be considered a major process since it conditioned an eventuality favouring a spontaneous biological and symbolic reunification of a human being affected in his integrity at a certain moment in his evolution (Dolto, 1957). Spontaneous biological and symbolic reunification is what Winnicott calls the dwelling of the psyche in the body and Dolto goes on to say that regression can occur when focused on the person of the therapist, that is to say organizable and accessible. The therapist thus becomes the complementary object for those who lack basic security in the unconscious image of their body (Dolto, 1957). This is a concept of regression that is very close to Winnicott's.

With his usual insistence, Winnicott even develops the idea that the analytic situation as set up by Freud, is itself a "drive to regression":

1. At a stated time daily, five or six times a week, Freud put himself at the service of the patient. (This time was arranged to suit the convenience of both the analyst and the patient.)
2. The analyst would be reliably there, on time, alive, breathing.
3. For the limited period of time prearranged (about an hour) the analyst would keep awake and become preoccupied with the patient.
4. The analyst expressed love by the positive interest taken, and hate in the strict start and finish and in the matter of fees. Love and hate were honestly expressed; that is to say, not denied by the analyst.
5. The aim of the analysis would be to get into touch with the process of the patient, to understand the material presented, to communicate this understanding in words. Resistance implied suffering and could be allayed by interpretation.
6. The analyst's method was one of objective observation.
7. This work was to be done in a room, not a passage, a room that was quiet and not liable to sudden unpredictable sounds, yet not dead quiet and not free from ordinary house noises. This room would be lit properly, but not by a light staring in the face, and not by a variable light. The room would certainly not be dark and it would be comfortably warm. The patient would be lying on a couch, that is to say, comfortable, if able to be comfortable, and probably a rug and some water would be available.
8. The analyst (as is well known) keeps moral judgement out of the relationship, has no wish to intrude with details of the analyst's personal life and ideas, and the analyst does not wish to take sides in the persecutory systems even when these appear in the form of real shared situations, local, political, etc. Naturally if there is a war or an earthquake or if the king dies, the analyst is not unaware.
9. In the analytic situation the analyst is much more reliable than people in ordinary life; on the whole punctual, free from temper tantrums, free from compulsive falling in love, etc.

10. There is a very clear distinction in the analysis between fact and fantasy, so that the analyst is not hurt by an aggressive dream.
11. An absence of the talion reaction can be counted on.
12. The analyst survives.

In this rather dated description we appreciate once more his particular sense of humour, and also the points he continues to insist on, in particular the importance of the reliability of the analyst. The description of an analytic setting with a reliable, present, punctual, living analyst refers of course to his theory of the function of the "mother-environment" at the very beginning, and can only elicit hope of accomplishing what had failed before. He points out that what is essential at that moment is the *capacity of the analyst to allow himself to be used as a subjective object*, his ability to be totally present, even without speaking or moving, since for the patient it will perhaps be the first time he will be able to experience the "capacity to be alone"; that is, alone in the presence of another person who is neither intrusive nor absent. From the start, he asserts that this capacity is one of the most important indications of the maturation of emotional development.

However, this possibility is not evident. The capacity to be alone, in the sense of real solitude, is founded in the infant's experience of relating to another. This other does not only remain at the right distance, but offers at the right time the ego support that allows experiences to be contained, which might otherwise lead to certain annihilation. Furthermore, "at the right distance" implies the minimum possible impingement, which allows the *infans* to "be" and not to react. And finally, ego support designates the task of metabolization which gives meaning to the instinctual experience felt by the baby.

And so the support provided by the mother's ego is like a canvas on which are drawn instinctual experiences. It is within this, and only this framework that the drive experiences will strengthen the ego of the infant.

> It is only when alone (that is to say, in the presence of someone) that the infant can discover his own personal life. [...] The infant is able to become unintegrated, to flounder, to be in a state in which there is no orientation, to be able to exist for a time without being either a reactor to an external impingement or an active person with a direction of interest or movement.
> (Winnicott, 1958/1964: 34)

The stage is then set to experience the "id": "In the course of time there arrives a sensation or an impulse. In this setting the sensation or impulse will feel real and be truly a personal experience" (Winnicott, 1958/1964). And from our point of view, it is the neutral reliability of the environment that ensures the conditions for these processes to exist and unfold in a meaningful way. It is therefore a state of solitude and quiet non-integration, with no threat of annihilation, for there is "someone" there who contains the situation.

> A large number of such experiences form the basis for a life that has reality in it instead of futility. This individual who has developed the capacity to be alone is constantly able to rediscover the personal impulse, and the personal impulse is not wasted because the state of being alone is something which (though paradoxically) always implies that someone else is there.
> (Winnicott, 1958/1964)

And so the capacity to be alone, which is, as we have seen, far from being acquired automatically, implies that the individual may have been able to establish an internal world beforehand, to recover a state of mental non-integration (that is, a state where he can "let himself be", a state of rest from the transitional space). The framework of the cure must be the place where the patient can experiment and rediscover this capacity to be alone, the indispensable grounds for an ability to relate to others.

Silence and regression

Winnicott constantly insists that a patient in regression needs to see that the analyst simply accepts his state, without necessarily bombarding him with interpretations, even if they are correct. Any interpretation will act as an impingement, causing the self to "react" and not just "be".

During the analytic hour there can sometimes be moments of regression lasting a few minutes, and sometimes there can even be a slight drowsiness. Instead of being considered an aggressive act, this drowsiness demonstrates precisely something of the capacity to be alone with the other, which we have mentioned. Only a feeling of security and experience of a safe framework will allow a patient to let him or herself fall asleep for a few seconds or minutes.

At times like these, adds Winnicott, the analyst is working with his "body ego".

> In one vitally important hour near the beginning of such a treatment I remained and knew I must remain absolutely still, only breathing. This I found very difficult indeed, especially as I did not yet know the special significance of the silence to my patient. At the end the patient came round from the regressed state and said: "Now I know you can do my analysis."
> (Winnicott, 1954a: 290)

This example, which is as banal as it is invaluable, reminds us that these states can represent one or several moments in the course of a session or group of sessions. Let us put aside the phantasmagoria of a regression that occupies all the sessions for weeks and weeks. This caricature lets us eliminate a key question: as Lacan let fly at Wladimir Granoff, "it is not babies who are babbling on your couch" (Granoff, 2001) – which is a roundabout way to understand that, for the patient, it is a return to a non-integrated state (prior to the integration) that may entail considerable risks.

Winnicott proposes another example, a little different but similar, in which he describes a woman patient who was so deeply regressed, in such a state of regression on the couch, that he did not know if she was alive or dead. He was in a panic. So he concentrated himself on her breathing – he compared her breathing to that of a bird – and by aligning his own rhythm with that of his patient, he continued breathing for a sustained period of time. By describing this somewhat extreme example, he effectively insists on the fact that all he could do was follow the rhythm of his patient and in particular, her breathing, which related to life. Finally Winnicott stresses that in the phases of deep regression, verbal interpretation is less important than the analytic situation as a whole. Once again, the state of deep regression implies a return to dependence and to the process of primitive development – psychic processes and not regressive body acting-out on the couch. The rest is but caricature and one or two examples that we would qualify as "limit" have served to discredit this process, which is actually extremely demanding for the analyst.

"The regressed patient is near to a reliving of dream and memory situation; an acting out of a dream may be the way the patient discovers what is urgent" (Winnicott, 1954a: 288). Of course this view underlines the theory that the patient has no access at that moment to the symbolization, and can only communicate through acting out. It is then up to the analyst, in a second phase, to give meaning to what has just happened. If he feels that this acting out is a hysterical outburst or a provocation, the patient will not be able to use it in any way, and the moment will be lost forever.

Withdrawal and regression

Winnicott relates thus an acting out of one of his patients – whose analysis is reported in detail in "Fragment of an Analysis" (Winnicott, 1989a: 19). The first incident occurred at the very start of the analysis. The patient rolled up in a ball and fell off the couch – this sort of thing had already happened during a previous analysis and had been interpreted by the analyst as a hysterical performance. While this was happening, Winnicott remains silent, but thinks that this action should be regarded as the first sign of a spontaneous self. Several sessions later, the patient declares that he sees himself doing the same thing – *he saw himself doing it*, but he didn't do it.

Winnicott goes on:

> The next withdrawn moment occurred a few weeks later. He had just made an attempt to use me as a substitute for his father (who had died when the patient was 18) and he asked me my advice about a detail in his work. I had first of all discussed this detail with him, pointing out, however, that he needed me as an analyst and not as a father-substitute. He had said it would be a waste of time to go on talking in his ordinary way, and then said that he had become withdrawn and felt this as a flight from something. [...] It was at this point that he just managed to tell me that he had again had the idea of being curled up, although in actual fact the was lying on his back as usual, with his hands together across his chest. It is here that I made the first of the interpretations which I know I would not have made twenty years ago. This interpretation turned out to be highly significant. When he spoke of being curled up, he made movement with his hands to show his curled-up position was somewhere in front of his face and that he was moving around in the curled-up position. I immediately said to him: In speaking of yourself as curled-up and moving around, you are at the same time implying something which naturally you are not describing since you are not aware of it ; you imply the *existence of a medium*. [...] He said, "like the

oil in which wheels move". [...] Following this the patient had a very important dream, and the analysis of this showed that he had been able to discard a shield, which was now no longer necessary since I had proved myself capable of supplying a suitable medium at the moment of his withdrawal.

He now began to sink more deeply into the analytic situation. [...] Much deeper material now emerged and he felt that there were people going in and out of the doors; my interpretation that this was associated with breathing was supported by further associations on his part. Ideas are like breath; also they are like children, and if I do nothing to them he feels they are abandoned. His great fear is of the abandoned child or the abandoned idea or remark, or the wasted gesture of a child.

(Winnicott, 1954b: 259)

What is more, the patient was suffering from a severe headache. Winnicott interpreted this pain situated to the exterior of the head as representing his need to have someone hold his head, as if he were a child in a state of deep emotional distress. "It was important that I did not hold his head actually, and in fact, as this would have been a mechanical application of technical principles. *The important thing was that I understood immediately what he needed*" (Winnicott, 1954b: 260).

This passage revises somewhat the ideas relating to the debate concerning physical contact with patients. The holding can only be metaphoric. We know that Margaret Little recalls in her account of her cure with Winnicott, that he was able to hold her hands for hours, during her moments of deep regression. This was in no way common practice for him. He always maintained that the empathetic understanding of the patient's profound anxiety should be conveyed in words, at the right moment. But we have already seen that in certain moments of regression, silence is necessary. Any intervention, even a clearing of the throat, would risk interrupting the process in progress. This example is an opportunity for Winnicott to illustrate the difference between withdrawal and regression. He states that the patient described in "Fragment of an Analysis" did not regress totally from a clinical point of view: "His regressions were localized in momentary withdrawal states with occurred in the analytic sessions" (Winnicott, 1954b: 255). And since the analyst had put into words these short-lived retreats, he could transform them into regressive episodes which became very positive for the patient. And he goes on to say that the patient "sinks deep into the analytic situation; on important but rare occasions he becomes withdrawn" (Winnicott, 1954b: 256). During these moments of retreat, unexpected things can occur, which he is sometimes able to relate, like the anecdote referred to.

> The idea behind this communication is that if we know about regression in the analytic hour, we can meet it immediately and in this way enable certain patients who are not too ill to make the necessary regressions in short phases, perhaps even almost momentarily. I would say that *in the withdrawn state the patient is holding the self* and that if immediately the withdrawn state appears *the analyst can hold the patient*, then what would otherwise have been a withdrawal state becomes a regression. The advantage of a *regression* is that it carries with it the opportunity for correction of inadequate adaptation-to-need in the past history of the patient, that is to say, in the patient's infancy management. By contrast, the *withdrawn* state is not profitable and when the patient recovers from a withdrawn state he or she is not changed.
>
> (Winnicott, 1954b: 261)

It means that the state of withdrawal or retreat remains sterile and, at that point, it is the skill of the analyst that transforms a brief state of withdrawal or retreat into something like regression, since he will have been able to offer the adequate holding which allows the patient to abandon the omnipotence of the false self. He goes on to state that:

> A patient curls up on the couch and rests the head on the hand and seems warm and contented. The rug is right over the head. The patient is alone. Of course we are used to all varieties of angry withdrawal, but the analyst has to be able to recognize this *regressive* withdrawal in which he is not being insulted but is being used in a very primitive and positive way.
>
> (Winnicott, 1954a: 289)

He concludes that regression reaches a level where it provides a starting place from which to operate. It permits the creation of a place where modifications appear possible or simply a return to the place where the situation had been frozen. The subject is in touch with the basic "self" processes that make up true development, and all that happens from then on appears real. It is about the *hic et nunc* of the analytic hour. It is not a re-reading of the past, nor a repetition, nor a remembering, nor a working-through, but something which can happen as it never has before. This gives full meaning to Winnicott's expression "Not yet experienced trauma". Something happened in the past which could not find a place to be inscribed – no place, since the subject was not there, not yet. It is what I called "void trauma". Therefore how to inscribe something which has not happened, but which is missing: its absence has brought about a distortion in the course of the development of the psychic apparatus? In short, something happens in the analytical hour, something perhaps which had never taken place. A psychic event takes place, where the process of unfreezing can be restarted. And behind these words we find the definition of the "act of analysis", a rewarding moment, of creation in the here and now.

References

Dolto, Françoise. 1957. "L'agressivité chez le jeune enfant", in *L' Évolution psychiatrique*, fascicule 3.
Granoff, Wladimir. 2001. *Lacan, Ferenczi et Freud*, Paris, Gallimard.
Lacan, Jacques. 1967–1968. *Le Séminaire, L'acte analytique 1967–1968*, unpublished.
Laplanche, Jean and Pontalis, Jean-Bertrand. 1967. *Vocabulaire de la psychanalyse*, Paris, PUF.
Winnicott, Donald W. 1954a. "Metapsychological and Clinical Aspects of Regression within the Psycho-Analytical Set-Up", in *Through Paediatrics to Psychoanalysis*, London, Karnac Books, or in *The Collected Works of D.W. Winnicott*, vol. 4.
Winnicott, Donald W. 1954b. "Withdrawal and Regression", in *Through Paediatrics to Psychoanalysis*, London, Karnac Books, or in *The Collected Works of D.W. Winnicott*, vol. 4.
Winnicott, Donald W. 1958/1964. "The Capacity to be Alone", in *The Maturational Processes and the Facilitating Environment*, London, Karnac Books, or in *The Collected Works of D.W. Winnicott*, vol. 5.
Winnicott, Donald W. 1963a. "Dependence in Infant-Care, in Child-Care and in the Psycho-Analytic Setting", in *The Maturational Processes and the Facilitating Environment*, London, Karnac Books, or in *The Collected Works of D.W. Winnicott*, vol. 6.
Winnicott, Donald W. 1963b. "Psychiatric Disorder in Terms of Infantile Maturational Processes", in *The Maturational Processes and the Facilitating Environment*, London, Karnac Books, or in *The Collected Works of D.W. Winnicott*, vol. 6.

Winnicott, Donald W. 1989a. "Fragment of an Analysis", in *Holding and Interpretation*, London, Karnac Books, or in *The Collected Works of D. W. Winnicott*, vol. 4.

Winnicott, Donald W. 1989b. "Ideas and Definitions", in *Psycho-Analytic Explorations*, London, Karnac Books, or in *The Collected Works of D. W. Winnicott*, vol. 9.

Chapter 9

The area of playing in the cure

The study we have developed here leads us logically to take interest in Winnicott's conception of the position of the analyst in the work of the cure. In the article "Transitional Objects and Transitional Phenomena", he concludes a long and very remarkable clinical vignette by this phrase: "In this session we had roamed over the whole field between subjectivity and objectivity, and we ended up with a bit of a game" (Winnicott, 2005b: 25). This phrase is somewhat surprising. It reminds us of the special place in human activity that Winnicott devotes to play. According to him, it is by playing that the human being can establish a rapport with the world and with himself. This experience begins with play at the breast, which means that the mother places her breast in such a way that "it's her nipple that the baby creates" (Winnicott, 1999: 103). Thus the baby can be active in the satisfaction of his needs and become the creator of the object that he has just discovered, and the need is transformed into desire. The successful repetition of these moments gives the baby the illusion of magical control over the creation of the object of desire and he can therefore bear its absence. This is how the infant creates and recreates the world at will, and "starts on the task at least as early as at the time of birth and of the theoretical first feed" (Winnicott, 1999: 110). It is the playful interaction between mother and baby. Playing is the direct successor of this period of illusion. As a result, the entire existence of mankind is built on the basis of playing. Playing is a creative experience, an experience that lies in the space-time continuum, a basic form of living. As we have already said, to play is to live.

Clare Winnicott recounts this anecdote:

> Many years ago a visitor staying in our home looked round thoughtfully and said: "You and Donald *play*." I remember

being surprised at this new light that had been thrown on us. We had certainly never *set out* to play; there was nothing self-conscious and deliberate about it. It seems just to have happened that we lived that way, but I could see what the visitor meant. We played with *things* – our possessions – rearranging, acquiring, and discarding according to our mood. We played with ideas, tossing them about at random.

(C. Winnicott, 1989: 14)

Winnicott notes: "in playing, and perhaps only in playing, the child or adult is free to be creative" (Winnicott, 1971: 53). He even goes so far as to comment on consultations with children: "If the therapist cannot play, then he is not suitable for the work. If the patient cannot play, then something needs to be done to enable the patient to become able to play, after which psychotherapy may begin" (Winnicott, 1971: 54). In fact, playing is of great importance, since it is only by playing that the patient can be creative, and living and playing are inseparable. Further reading of this clinical vignette pinpoints the fact that, just as with the squiggle game, the essential aspect is an exchange, not in the classical sense, ordinary and conversational, but due to the setting up of an intermediate space, an in-between area, an area of playing, perhaps the area of our greatest truth. Each person can outline or sketch a line which the other person can continue as his own creation. It is still a squiggle – this illegible signature – but a verbal squiggle. And just as he has shown in a squiggle session with children, there is often at the end of the session, a final moment, a moment of quiet reassurance, before the patient leaves the room.

And he contends that his statement regarding consultations with children is also valid in adult cures. "Psychotherapy takes place in the overlap of two areas of playing, that of the patient and that of the therapist. Psychotherapy has to do with two people playing together" (Winnicott, 1968: 38). And he goes on to say:

> the matter is more difficult to describe when the patient's material appears mainly in terms of verbal communication. I suggest that we must expect to find playing just as evident in the analyses of adults as it is in the case of our work with children. It manifests itself, for instance, in the choice of words, in the inflection of the voice, and indeed in the sense of humour.
>
> (Winnicott, 1968: 40)

But there is something about playing that has not found its place in psychoanalytical literature.

Openness and creativity are vital ingredients in the therapeutic process. If this creativity is reflected as a mirror image – and only if it is reflected – it integrates the individual, organized personality, and in the end it is this creativity that allows the individual to be and to be found (Winnicott, 2005a). A complex derivative of the face reflects what is there to be seen, except that the mirror is not a flat surface, but another human being. To understand this important and iconoclastic aspect, we must remember that psychoanalysis at that moment is submerging the patient with interpretations, however brilliant they may be. Whenever a patient expresses disagreement, he is said to be resisting. We have several attestations of this, for example Margaret Little's account of her analysis with Ella Sharpe (Little, 1992).

The ethic of reserve

Winnicott's approach is from the outset very different. He asks the analyst to adopt a position of effacement that we could call ethical. As the years go by, he intervenes less and less. It is interesting to follow the evolution of his style of working in relation to the patient whose cure he recounts in "Fragment of an Analysis" (D.W. Winnicott, 1989: 19). At the beginning of his work he bombards the patient with diverse interpretations:

> It appals me to think how much deep change I have prevented or delayed in patients in a certain classification category by my personal need to interpret. [...] I think I interpret mainly to let the patient know the limits of my understanding.
> (Winnicott, 1994: 86)

He declares to another patient: "I am silent because I don't know what to say" (Winnicott, 2005b: 24), to which she replies that it is fine, that she is satisfied and that she would have preferred that he say nothing at all. The reason the analyst intervenes, when he does say something, is not to show his knowledge, but to give the patient the possibility to access his real desire, when he feels the time is right. In this way, the analyst does not direct the cure,[1] but remains in a waiting position, one of respect and total receptivity but at the same time of complete vigilance. He has to be there, next to the patient, by his side, to be able to help him find the way through (as if they were clearing the undergrowth). It is about finding the way together, but the analyst must not lead, he accompanies, helping the creative act, and even perhaps indicating the direction, or showing hesitation in front of a path that leads nowhere. In order to do this, the analyst uses a form of subtle communication which runs the risk of going unnoticed. But this is not important. The procedure will take more time, and will need one or two deviations, but the journey will continue. On the other hand, a dogmatic interpretation, however correct and brilliant it might be, will – if we use the same metaphor – have the effect of immobilizing the progression or make it take another direction.

Winnicott feels that every patient is equipped with a creative potential that is fuelled, nourished by each intervention from the analyst. One of his patients said to him one day: "Good management (ego care) such as I have experienced during this hour is a feed (id-satisfaction)". The analyst explains that his patient could not have made himself understood by inversing the phrase, for "he could not have said this the other way round, for if I had fed him he would have complied and this would have played into his False Self defence" (Winnicott, 1960: 140–141). We cannot imagine that the objective pursued – the development of creativity in the patient – could be arrived at by a doctrinal, or even informative intervention by the analyst. For once again it is the introduction of the issue of the found-created. The psychoanalyst "sows the seed" of ideas in the transitional area between himself and the patient, ideas that will remain dormant, like seeds which germinate long after their sowing, when all hope of seeing them grow has disappeared. They can only be "used" when the patient is ready to accept and integrate them, in order to resolve his internal problem. They will then become one of his "possessions", in the same way that the baby possesses the breast. They were there, waiting to be found. Of course it is because they were there that they were able to be created and then found; the patient can use them as necessary in his own creative space. It is a precious moment when the patient makes a personal discovery of something which had already been suggested without success and left long dormant, something integrated and mutative. This process throws light on what Winnicott calls "the use of the analyst", which in reality describes the use *by the patient* of the analytic situation.

> Our patients teach us these things, and it is distressing to me that I must give these views as if they were my own. All analysts have

this difficulty, and in a sense it is more difficult for an analyst to be original than for everyone else, because everything that we say truly has been taught us yesterday, apart from the fact that we listen to each other's papers and discuss matters privately. In our work, especially in working on the schizoid rather than the psychoneurotic aspects of the personality, we do in fact wait, if we feel we know, until the patients tell us, and in doing so creatively make the interpretation we might have made; if we make the interpretation out of our own cleverness and experience then the patient must refuse it or destroy it. An anorexia patient is teaching me the substance of what I am saying now as I write it down.

(Winnicott, 1963a: 182)

Our role is that of waiting. "If only we can wait, the patient arrives at understanding creatively and with immense joy, and I now enjoy this joy more than I used to enjoy the sense of having been clever" (Winnicott, 1994: 219). But waiting does not mean being inactive or asleep. It means tolerating and accepting the moments of pause, at the same time maintaining the appropriate environment which was missing at the start.

This method of working proves particularly necessary in the case of patients who use a perpetual intellectualization of their experience. If this type of personality undertakes a cure with an impersonal and generally silent analyst, but who from time to time makes correct interpretations, it will only strengthen the collusion with the patient's false self. There is a risk that the patient and the analyst will enter into a never-ending process. Everything seems fine. Both of them feel intelligent, each is pleased with the other. But no real analytical work is accomplished.[2]

The non-intrusion by the analyst is a vital element in allowing the process to unfold itself completely. This has been one of Winnicott's favourite themes, ever since "The Observation of Infants in a Set Situation", a situation that is often simply called "the spatula baby" – a text dating from 1941.

Creating an emotional bridge

We saw in the preceding chapter the importance Winnicott gave to the use of regression in the psychoanalytical process. The non-intrusion assumes that the intervention by the analyst only serves to encourage the process of personal discovery. In this kind of situation, the analyst must be very careful about the words he uses. Winnicott states that ultimately what is important is not what is said, but the way in which it is said. For there is a subtle interplay between vocabulary and syntax, so that, just like the squiggle game, the interventions are simply a method of continuation, a gentle encouragement to continue – never adopting a directive nature. They represent something that allows thought to develop without feeling compliant, and without being on the defensive, and they are subtle enough for the patient to be able to disregard them without his personal creativity being affected.

Bob's squiggle has shown us that occasionally the analyst gambles. This is done in such a way that the patient cannot avoid taking him up on it, but without it putting his personal process in danger by an impingement on his psychic space. So what has to be invented is a "non-polluting" language, not contaminated by the analyst's own associations; to recover the patient's own words, like an echo amplifying some aspects more than others, would leave open and unresolved a continuation towards another area. It means speaking the language of the part of the patient that is present, and which is at that moment in communication with his other. So for a patient in their childhood phase who uses the terms "Daddy" and "Mummy", the analyst must try to get to a moment in the session when he can say "your father" and "your mother", thus repositioning them both structurally. The opposite is just as true. Occasionally it seems appropriate to go back to the terms used in the patient's childhood. The use of these little nicknames allows us to address the child still present in the adult, indirectly of course. We can also voluntarily use colloquial words or slang, which is all the more disconcerting when the analyst is expected to speak in a more mannered fashion. For example: "Oh that's really shitty", during a session which is dealing with anal material. Once again, the importance lies in the fact that the process of the patient's evolution must not be contaminated. If the patient at that particular moment can take over this language and use it, he will not feel hindered in following his own path. He will leave the session remembering how his analyst had used bad language or a silly play on words that day, but this "liberty" will be without consequence and will perhaps later bear fruit.

All these examples show us the importance of creating an "emotional bridge" in the context of a regression in time. When he or she hears these words again, it will allow emotion and feelings felt as a child to be relived, while experiencing their problem, and allows them to manage the integration of these memories with the affect associated with it.

And Winnicott emphasizes that we cannot ignore the importance in the cure of humour and laughter.[3] The sense of humour is part of the freedom of the game of verbal squiggle, a play on words which can bring a lighter touch and bonding, and which can sometimes alleviate a highly emotional situation. Humour is a way of symbolizing metaphorically that which had not been dealt with before, thus avoiding the complexity of a classical interpretation. Humour provides an aid to the setting up of an area of fantasy.

Winnicott maintains that a burst of laughter during a session is like the "poetic moment" that exists between the baby and the mother. Of course the difference depends on whether it comes from the analyst or the patient. On the analyst's side it can have the value of an interpretation, and once again it can represent a way of signifying, which even if not understood, will not perturb the progress. From the patient's side, it is often a sign of the emergence of an area of truth. It is an enactment which gives a meaning. "It's the sign of the removal of an unconscious obstacle" according to Octave Mannoni (1985: 193), who regrets that this particular kind of play is not used in the cure often enough. As for Freud, he maintained that his patients laughed each time they were on the point of discovering something unconscious. And as we have seen with the squiggle game, the vital moment is when the patient is surprised.

Generally speaking, the importance lies in the use that the patient makes of both the setting and the analyst. Winnicott writes:

> *The patient makes use of the analyst's failures.* Failures there must be, and indeed there is no attempt to give perfect adaptation. [...] Others may be surprised, as I was, to find that while a gross mistake may do but little harm, a very small error of judgment may produce a big effect.
>
> (Winnicott, 1955: 298)

Winnicott constantly reminds us that what caused the illness is the failure of the environment at a very early stage, at a period when the *infans* did not possess the necessary equipment to deal with them in terms of projection. And above all, these failures were unpredictable. Currently, the analyst can provoke his own failures, so that the patient can recapture the early deprivation, which is still there, and at last express his/her anger. Winnicott writes: "The clue is that the analyst's failure is being used and must be treated as a *past* failure" (Winnicott, 1955: 298).

The analyst must recognize and accept these failures: "The analyst needs to be able to make use of this failure in terms of their meaning for the patient, and he must if possible account for each failure even if this means a study of his unconscious countertransference." And he goes on to say:

> The operative factor is that the patient now hates the analyst for the failure that originally came as an environmental factor, outside the infant's area of omnipotent control, but that is now staged in the transference. So in the end, we succeed by failing – failing the patient's way.
> (Winnicott, 1963b: 258)

Therefore the analyst uses his own errors in his work, and it is they that justify the objective anger of the patient. As a consequence we can understand the sense of the claim that an unsuccessful analysis is a fiasco not because of the patient but because of the analyst.

What we have just described does not concern the episodes of deep regression that we evoked in the preceding chapter. In these particular moments, "what matters is not what the analyst does, but what he is". This phrase is at the very least questionable, and demands much humility on our part for it is not the analyst who has the knowledge, it is the patient. The least that we can expect from an analyst is that he will not obstruct the analysis. In this sense Winnicott lists the non-verbal messages included in his approach to the patient – the tone of voice, a warm or cool reception, a rigid or relaxed corporal attitude – at the same time as the words themselves. He specifies: "Nevertheless, every analyst knows that along with the content of interpretation this attitude is reflected in the nuances and in the timing and in a thousand ways to compare with the infinite variety of poetry" (Winnicott, 1987: 95–96).

At these particular moments in the cure – which as we know are not the most frequent – any intervention by the analyst would risk interrupting the process underway.

> In this kind of work we know that even the right explanation is ineffectual. The person we are trying to help needs a new

experience in a specialized setting. The experience is one of a non-purposive state, as one might say a sort of ticking over of the unintegrated personality.
(Winnicott, 2005a: 169–179)

In "Playing: Creative Activity and the Search for the Self" (Winnicott, 1971: 53), he describes a session with a woman that lasted three hours in which it seems that his patient let herself go into a state of non-integration and to a succession of "nonsensical" words and activities, nonsense that he does not try to interpret, for "organized nonsense" is already a defence, just as organized chaos is a denial of chaos. Winnicott is careful not to intervene, and relieves his mind by writing down interpretations, which he withholds! It is important to read this strange and disconcerting session, for at the end the patient herself makes the interpretation that he withheld. Therefore in the analytical set up, there is no "expert who knows" and "patient who does not know". There is creation in the *hic et nunc* of the transitional area of a new knowledge, a knowledge "otherwise". An inaugural or seminal moment?

> In my clinical work I have proved, at least to myself, that one kind of analysis does not preclude the other. I find myself slipping over from one to the other and back again, according to the trend of the patient's unconscious process. [...] What needs to be done now is the study in detail of the criteria by which the analyst may know when to work with the change of emphasis, how to see that a need is arising which is of the kind that I have said must be met (at least in a token way) by active adaptation.
> (Winnicott, 1955: 299)

This conception of the cure allows the patients to liberate themselves from a sustained dependence, contrary to what we may have thought. The satisfaction of a need liberates, whereas with desire, we can engage in a never-ending demand. Psychotherapy is not about giving clever and shrewd interpretations.

> It is a long-term giving the patient back what the patient brings. [...] I like to think of my work this way, and to think that if I do this well enough the patient will find his or her own self, and will be able to exist and to feel real.
> (Winnicott, 1967: 158)

Winnicott was an incurable optimist, as we have already said. Let us leave him the final word: "Psychoanalysis is no way of life. We all hope that our patients will finish with us and forget us, and that they will find living itself to be the therapy that makes sense" (Winnicott, 1994: 220).

Notes

1 Will we ever be able to find another term than "directing the cure"?
2 On the particular question of the false self, see Dethiville (2014).
3 Winnicott had a great sense of humour and often used it. This sometimes leads to a misunderstanding of his texts for non-English speakers, for whom these little flashes of humour, which the English spot immediately, are not obvious in the written text.

References

Dethiville, Laura. 2014. *Donald W. Winnicott: A New Approach*, London, Karnac Books.
Little, Margaret. 1992. *Des États-limites: L'alliance thérapeutique*, Paris, Éditions des Femmes.
Mannoni, Octave. 1985. "Le rire", in *Le Moi et l'autre*, Paris, Denoël.
Winnicott, Clare. 1989. "D.W.W: A Reflection", in *Psychoanalytic Explorations*, London, Karnac Books, or in *The Collected Works of D.W. Winnicott*, vol. 12.
Winnicott, Donald W. 1955. "Clinical Varieties of Transference", in *Through Paediatrics to Psychoanalysis*, London, Karnac Books, or in *The Collected Works of D.W. Winnicott*, vol. 5.
Winnicott, Donald W. 1963a. "Communicating and Not Communicating, Leading to a Study of Certain Opposites", in *The Maturational Processes and the Facilitating Environment*, London, Routledge, or in *The Collected Works of D.W. Winnicott*, vol. 6.
Winnicott, Donald W. 1963b. "Dependence in Infant-Care, in Child-Care and in the Psycho-Analytic Setting", in *The Maturational Processes and the Facilitating Environment*, London, Karnac Books, or in *The Collected Works of D.W. Winnicott*, vol. 6.
Winnicott, Donald W. 1960. "Ego Distortion in Terms of True and False Self", in *The Maturational Processes and the Facilitating Environment*, London, Karnac Books, or in *The Collected Works of D.W. Winnicott*, vol. 6.
Winnicott, Donald W. 1967. "Mirror-Role of Mother and Family in Child Development", in *Playing and Reality*, London, Routledge, or in *The Collected Works of D.W. Winnicott*, vol. 8.

Winnicott, Donald W. 1968. "Playing: A Theoretical Statement", in *Playing and Reality*, London, Routledge, or in *The Collected Works of D.W. Winnicott*, vol. 8.

Winnicott, Donald W. 1971. "Playing: Creative Activity and the Search for the Self", in *Playing and Reality*, London, Routledge, or in *The Collected Works of D.W. Winnicott*, vol. 8.

Winnicott, Donald W. 1987. "Communication Between Infant and Mother, and Mother and Infant, Compared and Contrasted", in *Baby and Their Mothers*, Reading, MA, Addison-Wesley, or in *The Collected Works of D.W. Winnicott*, vol. 8.

Winnicott, Donald W. 1989. "Fragment of an Analysis", in *Holding and Interpretation*, London, Karnac Books, or in *The Collected Works of D.W. Winnicott*, vol. 4.

Winnicott, Donald W. 1994. "The Use of an Object and Relating through Identification", in *Playing and Reality*, London, Routledge, or in *The Collected Works of D.W. Winnicott*, vol. 8.

Winnicott, Donald W. 1999. "Establishment of Relationship with External Reality" in *Human Nature*, London, Free Association Books, or in *The Collected Works of D.W. Winnicott*, vol. 11.

Winnicott, Donald W. 2005a. *Playing and Reality*, London, Routledge, or in *The Collected Works of D.W. Winnicott*, vol. 8.

Winnicott, Donald W. 2005b. "Transitional Objects and Transitional Phenomena", in *Playing and Reality*, London, Routledge, or in *The Collected Works of D.W. Winnicott*, vol. 3.

Index

Abram, Jan 39
addictions 93
adolescence 81–94; addictions in 93; antisocial tendency 56, 61; auto-destruction 46; crisis of 86; delinquency 56, 92–94; destructiveness 87; doldrums in 43, 81, 83–84, 92, 93; dreams 91; and fathers 34–35; isolation 89–92; parents' regression to own 82–83; and play 91; sexuality and 87; and siblings 47; squiggle game and 23; transference 89; the unconscious 87; World Wars and 81–82
"adolescent paranoia" 89
aggression 68–79; adolescence and 87; antisocial tendency and 52, 55; and blocking 98; death instinct and 75; deprivation and 58; hate 76–79; inherent 52; primary instinctive motricity 68–72; and projection 70, 78
Aggression and its Relation to Emotional Development (Winnicott) 68
analyst, identification to parental figure 89
annihilation: breastfeeding and 69, 70; primitive agony 69, 75; and regression 98, 101–102, 105–106
anorexia 47, 117
antipsychiatry movement 39
antisocial tendency 50–67; and adequate environment 56–57; and adolescence 56, 61; delinquency 50, 56, 65–67; and deprivation 50–56; destructiveness 53–54, 57; evacuated children 61–65; and integration 55; and play 55; and projection 50; regression 57–61; and sign of hope 52–53, 65–67
anxiety 18, 46, 55
"Aspects of Regression in the Analytic Set-Up" conference 1954 103
auto-destruction 46, 79, 87
availability of analysis 6
Avello, José Jiménez 76

Balint, Michael 96
bed-wetting 52, 60
Bion, Wilfred R. 71, 101
blocking: and aggression 78; and family 48; of maturation 64; and regression 96, 98
Boorman, John 61–62
Bowlby, John 51, 63, 66
breastfeeding 29–30, 113
British Medical Journal 63n1
British Psychoanalytical School 74
British Psychoanalytical Society 63
Britton, Clare 66
Brook, Peter 62

cathexis 21
"The Child in the Family Group" (Winnicott) 38
Children's Act 1948 66

Index

Cinderella 46
Clancier, Anne 4–5
CMPP (*Centre medico-psycho-pédagogique*) 87
communication, ease of 4
"communication of significance" 15, 17
"Contemporary Concepts of Adolescent Development and their Implications for Higher Education" (Winnicott) 81
Cooper, David 39
countertransference 97–98, 120
creativity 15, 18, 54, 72, 74, 115–116, 118
cross-communication 24
Curtis Committee 67

death instinct 74–76, 79
delinquency: adolescence 56, 92–94; evacuated children 63–65; as sign of hope 65–67; regression 57
"Delinquency as a Sign of Hope" conference 1967 50
dependence: absolute 65, 86; analyst as maternal figure 100; deprivation and 65; of infant 30; play and 121; relative 51, 64, 86; regression to 54, 98, 101–103, 107
depression, parental 10, 20, 22, 55; post-partum depression 28
deprivation, emotional: adult symptoms 52; and analyst's failure 119–120; and antisocial tendency 50–56; childhood symptoms 52–53; evacuated children 61–65; loss of parent 56–57; regression 58
Deprivation and Delinquency (Winnicott) 25, 88
"Deprived Mothers" (Winnicott) 61
"destruction of the object" 71
destructiveness: adolescence 87; antisocial tendency and 53–54, 57; father and 31–32, 35; pathological 73–74; positive 72–73; and the unconscious 79
Dethiville, Laura 2
detoxification 71

disintegration 10, 53, 65, 74, 99
distance, travelling 6
divorce and hope of reunion 38
doldrums: in adolescence 43, 81, 83–84, 92, 93; and squiggle game 16, 20
Dolto, Françoise 103–104
"double therapy" 9
dreams: in adolescence 91; and father 33; Freud and 89; and regression 99, 101, 107, 109; and "sacred moment" 11; and squiggle game 18, 19, 21
drive pressure 18
"D.W.W. on D.W.W." (Winnicott) 56

ego: and adolescence 86–89; and annihilation 98, 105; "body ego" 107; infant 71, 77, 105; and regression 99, 101
emotional bridge 117–122
environment: adequate 56–61, 71, 102; use of 8–11
envy 29, 81
expense of treatment 6

family 38–48; blocking and 48; as foundation 42; and individual creative activity 41–42; integration of 40–41, 42; loyalty and disloyalty 44–48; maturation and 44; multiple identification 41; as not psychoanalytic concept 39; privilege of 42, 44; and projection 44, 45; separations and reconciliations 43–45; siblings 45–48; and the unconscious 43
family background 8, 9
family games 45
father/paternal function 25–36; as arbitrator 32; and completeness 32–36; and destructiveness 31–32, 35; in French analysis 25, 31, 33, 35; idealization of 34; and identification 33; and integration 26, 33, 35; as maternal substitute 28, 30; and mother-environment 30–31; and movement 28; and play 28; post-partum depression

and role of 28; *prehistorical* 33; projection 34; and psychic reality 30; puerperal psychosis and role of 28; role of 26–29; symbolic father 35; as third person in relationship 28–30, 32–33; and the unconscious 29–30
Fear of Breakdown (Winnicott) 32
feminism 31, 32
Ferenczi, Sándor 75–76, 96
first interview 7
First World War 81
"Fragment of an Analysis" (Winnicott) 108–109, 115
frame 100–101
French analysis: and the father 25, 31, 33, 35; feminism 32; *see also* Dolto, Françoise; Lacan, Jacques
Freud, Sigmund: analyst as parental figure 89; "Beyond the Pleasure Principle" 74; and eath instinct 74–76; *The Ego and the Id* 33; on hate 77; and images 19; importance to Winnicott 23, 35; on laughter 119; on libido 69; *Moses and Monotheism* 26; on regression 96, 99, 103, 104

Geets, Claude 10
Golding, William 62
Granoff, Wladimir 107
group therapy, parents 20

Harry Potter (novels and films) 93–94
Hate in the Counter-Transference (Winnicott) 66
holding of analysis in regression 101, 109, 110
Hope and Glory (film) 61–62
humour, role of 119

id: and adolescence 86; in infants 56; regression 106
identification: of the analyst to parental figure 89; and father 33; multiple 41; projective 78
incest 35
independence 10, 98

"indestructible environment" 31–32, 35
integration: and antisocial tendency 55; ego-coverage of mother 87; of family 40–41, 42; and hate 76; play and 115, 116, 119; and regression 98, 101; role of father 26, 33, 35
Isaacs, Susan 66
introjection 32, 34

jealousy 29, 45, 46

Kalmanovitch, Jeanine 4–5
Khan, Masud 6
kidults 82
Klein, Melanie: and 'cruel infant' 68, 70; death instinct 74
Kleinian psychoanalysis 23
Kristeva, Julia 85

Lacan, Jacques 31, 40, 44, 54, 99, 107
Laing, Ronald 39
Laplanche, Jean 39, 96
laughter, role of 119
libido 69
life-instinct 75, 76
Little, Margaret 79, 115
London County Council 3
Lord of the Flies (novel and film) 62, 83

"madness" 8, 65; "healthy madness" 27
males, maternal 27
Mannoni, Octave 11n2, 85, 88, 119
maturation 44
McDougall, Joyce 5–6
"Metapsychological and Clinical Aspects of Regression Within the Psycho-Analytical Set-Up" (Winnicott) 99
Miller, Emmanuel 63
"The Mirror Role of Mother and Family in Child Development" (Winnicott) 19
mother: and adolescence 87; availability of 10; breast play

113; death of 55; depression in 20, 22; ego and 105; evacuated children 61–64; and family 40; hallucination of 58; hatred for baby 77–78; idealization of 45; importance of 8, 79; infant view of 33; and movement of baby 68–71; panic attacks in 20, 22; regression 99–101, 103; and role of father 25–30, 34, 35–36; and squiggle game 21–22; as subjective object 32
"mother-environment" 30–31, 53–54, 105
motricity, instinctive 68–72
Museum of Mankind, Paris, "The Thousand and One Ways to be Born" (*Naître ici et ailleurs*) exhibition 36

neurosis 8, 86
non-integration 106, 107, 121
non-intrusion by analyst 115–118, 120–121
non-verbal communication 101, 120

"The Observation of Infants in a Set Situation" ("The Observation of the Spatula Game") (Winnicott) 6, 117
Oedipus complex 35, 43, 46, 86
openness 115

Paddington Green Children's Hospital 3–5
panic attacks, maternal 22
paranoia 89
paternal function *see* father
pathological destruction 73–74
personality distortion 65
play 113–122; and adolescence 91; and antisocial tendency 55; emotional bridge 117–122; family and 42, 45; father and 28; and mental state 11; non-intrusion by analyst 115–117; and the unconscious 119; *see also* squiggle game
Playing and Reality (Winnicott) 68

"Playing: Creative Activity and the Search for the Self" (Winnicott) 121
Pontalis, J.B. 25, 39, 96
positive destructiveness 72–73
post-partum depression 28
"primary maternal preoccupation" 8, 27
"primitive agony" 48, 69, 75
projection: and aggression 70, 78; antisocial tendency 50; containment of 18; and father 34; family 44, 45
projective identification 78
psyche-soma 76, 98
psychic area 39
psychosomatic illness 102
psychosis 10, 65, 97, 99; puerperal psychosis 28
"Psychotherapeutic Interview with an Adolescent" (Winnicott) 88
puerperal psychosis 28

Queen Elizabeth Hospital for Children, Hackney 3

regression: 96–111; antisocial tendency 57–61; by parents of adolescents 82; frame of analysis 100–101; holding of analysis 101, 109, 110; integration and 98, 101; reliability of analyst 102–106; setting of analysis 101, 105, 106; and silence 106–108; and the unconscious 98, 104; and withdrawal 108–111
reintegration 23
reliability 102–106
Roustang, François 40

"sacred moment" 11, 18–19
Second World War: and adolescence 81–92; evacuation of children 61–65
setting of analysis in regression 101, 105, 106
sexuality: and adolescence 87; and breastfeeding 29; maternal 25
Shakespeare, William 82

siblings 45–48; parental role of 44
somatic disorders 3–4
somnambulistic state 59
space and "therapeutic consultation" 5
Spiegelman, Art 13
squiggle game 13–24; and age 23; as communication 15; and cross-communication 24; and doldrums 16, 20; freedom of thought 20; importance of last drawing 23; process and technique 14–18; as product of subconscious 19; as signature 20–24; verbal 114, 118–119
stealing 52, 53, 58, 60
stepmothers, evil in fiction 45–46
stepparents 44–47, 55
"Struggling through the Doldrums" (Winnicott) 81
the subconscious 19
"sub-deprivation" 54
subjective object: analyst as 11, 17, 18, 105; and destructiveness 72; mother as 32
suicide 88, 101
suicide attempts 38, 79, 91
superego 35
Systemic school of psychoanalysis 39

Thematic Apperception Test (T.A.T.) 14
"therapeutic consultation" 4–5, 7–11
Therapeutic Consultations in Child Psychiatry (Winnicott) 6, 8–9, 35, 41–42, 56
transference: and adolescence 89; and play 120; regression and 96, 97, 100, 101
transference dependence 102
"Transitional Objects and Transitional Phenomena" (Winnicott) 113

the unconscious: in adolescence 87; analyst's failure 120; and destructiveness 79; and evacuated children 64; and family 43; and the father 29–30; and play 119; regression 98, 104
"The Use of an Object in the Context of *Moses and Monotheism*" (Winnicott) 33

verbalization 23, 96

"What About Father?" (Winnicott) 27, 33
Winnicott, Clare 113–114
Winnicott, Donald: on adequate environment 57–61; on adolescence 81–85, 86, 87, 88, 90–92; on aggression 68–69; on analysis as art 8; on analyst's failures 119–120; on analyst's learning 18; on antisocial tendency 50–53, 55–56, 61, 65–66, 92; basic axiom of 17; and beginning of psychic life 70–71; on countertransference 97–98; on death instinct 75; definition of deprivation 51; on destructiveness 54, 60, 72–73; and evacuated children 63–66; on family 38–43, 45; on father 25–28, 30–35; on fear 48; on first interview 7; on hate 76–78; on his work 2, 3; on hope 20, 122; on non-intrusion 115–118, 120–121; on non-verbal messages of analyst 120; on parents 10; on play 11, 23, 113–114; on positive destructiveness 72–73; on regression 97–111; on squiggle game 13–14, 15, 16–17, 19–22; subjective object of 11; on wartime hostels 92–93; on withdrawal 108–109; work compared to music 7
The Winter's Tale (Shakespeare) 82
withdrawal 22, 51, 108–110

"Youth Will Not Sleep" (Winnicott) 82